To Alan and Avril

Very best wishes

on behalf of Tony

Kath and Gill

14 January 2009

WATER ON THE BRAIN
THE MEMOIRS OF TONY DOWNING

Water on the Brain

The Memoirs of Tony Downing

by

TONY DOWNING

The Memoir Club

© Tony Downing 2005

First published in 2005 by
The Memoir Club
Stanhope Old Hall
Stanhope
Weardale
County Durham

British Library Cataloguing in
Publication Data.
A catalogue record for this book
is available from the
British Library.

ISBN: 1 84104 119 X

Typeset by George Wishart & Associates, Whitley Bay.
Printed by CPI Bath.

Dedicated to Kath and Gill

Contents

Illustrations

Acknowledgements

The author would like to thank HM Stationery Office for the use of photographs 3, 7, 8, 9, 10, 11, 16 and 17.

Preface

BY CHANCE, as I was about to put pen to paper my eye fell on the cover of Clive James's *Unreliable Memoirs*. Clearly I've been pre-empted, I thought, because that would have been an appropriate title for this account. This is not because I've deliberately altered events and characters as Clive James says he has done, but essentially because I've never kept a diary and my memory of many past events has become badly blurred.

Indeed I believe I should not be exaggerating in concluding that I have now forgotten almost as much as I still remember. Even so, to keep this document to an acceptable length, I have been able to do no more than include what I hope is a representative selection of the events and personalities I've encountered in a 50-year working lifetime involving work on hundreds of projects and meeting thousands of people. Additionally, with the same objective of brevity in mind, I have concentrated, after the early years, almost entirely on my technical experiences, with just a few non-technical sidelights, omitting most of my social events prior to retirement a few years ago. Additionally I have kept technical jargon down to a minimum and omitted almost all flow sheets, equations, treatment plant configurations and model frameworks such as would normally dominate my publications. To anyone who has not been mentioned but who feels that he or she should have been and for any other inadvertent errors I humbly apologize.

Foreword

by **Professor Peter Wolf,**

Emeritus Professor of the City University, London

WHEN, Dr Tony Downing and I met by chance, at the Annual General Meeting of the Royal Academy of Engineering, and he invited me to write this foreword, I happily accepted because he is one of the most distinguished as well as delightfully companionable people in our business. Now that I have read the manuscript, I stand in awe of the man; a reader can tell at once that he is a friendly person, but nobody who had not met him could recognise from reading his memoirs what a professional giant he is.

I mentioned 'our business' and, like him, of course refer to *water*, the stuff we in Britain tend to take for granted. More than 85 years ago, I started playing in a little local stream, building little canals and earth dams and diverting little channels, and in essence I am still playing the same game. My special activity has been to find water in nature, where it is needed, and to protect the community from floods where too much of it threatens. Most of this means a preoccupation with the *quantity* of water, whereas Dr Downing has tended to deal with water *quality*, pollution and purification; but quality and quantity are closely linked in water supply for various purposes and in drainage. So it is not surprising that, about fifty years ago, I met his predecessor as Director of the government's Water Pollution Research Laboratory (WPRL), Dr B A Southgate, CBE, on government and learned-society research committees. These memoirs pay generous tribute to that great man whom I remember as a distinguished, powerful, assertive and impressive contributor to scientific discussions, who did not seem to approve of questions and clearly disliked contradiction.

Dr Downing tries to give the impression that much of his time was devoted to sport, the arts and social activities, but I have known him for over forty years as a hard-working, capable and diplomatic scientist and leader, so I am not surprised that Dr Southgate groomed him as his successor, both as head of the WPRL, and as a prominent member of research committees. Dr Downing's committee technique was always gentle, enquiring and encouraging, and at the same time authoritative when he was asked about his and his colleagues' work. The eminent prizes and awards conferred on him during his splendid career show that he has been held in high esteem in the UK and throughout the outside world. My own admiration is for his great contribution to government research and its management, to university teaching and research at the international course in the Netherlands at Delft and as a Visiting Professor in my own old Department at Imperial College in London, and above all for his brilliance as a partner of a world-class firm for whom I have also a few times been a consultant (never, alas, in his company). Until I read this manuscript, I had no idea of the range of his contributions; and noting the modesty of his presentation, I suspect that he does not give us a full account of all of them.

There is one important part of his story, which I found especially enlightening, namely his account of the re-organization of water research in England and Wales which led to his departure from government service. In 1973 and 1974, I was puzzled to find that there were a member of ordinary (not in my estimation extra-ordinarily meritorious) civil servants in the water world who, before the normal age of retirement, were allowed to retire and were given royal honours. The memoirs tell the story of how Dr Downing was subtly led to the point of offering his early resignation; in resigning, he proved himself to be the noblest and most unselfish member of a group of men who, at that time, were the leaders of national water research and development.

We owe him a great debt for his splendid scientific work and leadership, and I regret that he was not publicly recognized for his great contributions to public health. Reading these memoirs, I also realize how ignorant we, his professional colleagues, were nearly thirty years ago, and how remiss in not giving him our support.

The memoirs also confirm my impression that, during the past thirty years, government research in the water field has lost its leading position in the world.

To finish as I started, Tony Downing and his wife are most delightful people; we rarely meet, but when we do they are wonderful company. In addition to that, I salute Tony as a successor of Bazalgette in his great contribution first to the British and later to the world's public health.

London, November 2004   **P O Wolf**

CHAPTER 1

Early Years and Schooldays

I WAS BORN ON 27 March 1926 in Longton Infirmary, Staffordshire, the son of Sydney Arthur and Frances Dorothy Downing. My father was a roofing-tile manufacturer and my mother, his second wife, had been a schoolteacher. We lived in a house jocularly called 'Red Marley' (after the basic ingredient of the tiles) located on Barlaston Old Road, opposite the local golf course. At the time my father was quite wealthy, one of his prized possessions being a yellow and black Rolls-Royce Coupé. This had a shelf at the back on which I was often perched yelling, I'm told, 'Pass that car Daddy', irrespective of whether the car was travelling in the same or the opposite direction.

Sadly my memories of my father stem almost solely from family anecdotes and photographs since he died when I was four from heart failure following angina, at the young age of forty-five. Regretfully there were no such technologies as angioplasty or heart by-passes in those days, an observation I make with some poignancy because although presumably through inheritance I have suffered from the same complaint of clogged arteries, a triple by-pass in 1999 appears to have given me, in effect, a new lease of life.

My father had three daughters, Constance (Connie), Zena and Margaret, and a son, Sydney (Plate 1) by his first wife, and I came to have great affection for all of them. I have, however, no direct recollections of the rest of my father's family. I mention this only as a reason for my reliance on family statements to the effect that my second Christian name is Leighton because my paternal grandmother was Lord Leighton's niece.

My father had been in partnership with his elder brother, Harry, in

1

1. With 'big brother' Sydney c. 1935.

their firm, Downing's Chesterton Ltd, and my mother was convinced that after his death she had been deprived of an adequate share of my father's holding in the firm. Thus from being quite wealthy she became relatively poor. So certain was she that the alleged 'unscrupulous Uncle Harry', as she described him to me, had taken an undue proportion of my father's holding that she took legal action. Events, of which I have no clear recall, took some time to unfold but after about two or three years my mother obtained a favourable settlement. However this merely gave her only a little more than basic subsistence. Meanwhile Red Marley was sold, and my half-brother and half-sisters, who were by then in their late teens or early twenties, set up their own home. My mother took me to live with my grandparents (Albert and Harriet Smith) elsewhere in Trentham. It was there where I perpetrated the first of my more notable errors. I got off a bus which stopped near the front of the house and recklessly ran off behind it across the road. At least it would have been across the road had it not been for a car coming in the opposite direction which struck me and knocked me flying. Fortunately it must have been just a glancing blow because after a momentary dazed feeling I picked myself up and assured my mother that I was all right. She poor lady was in tears and it took her quite some time to recover after the event. I suffered not the slightest after-effect and I can only hope the same was true of the car driver.

My grandfather worked as a porcelain decorator for Copelands, who made Spode, and judging from the several pieces of Minton that I've inherited probably also did some work for that firm. Occasionally he would bring home pieces (seconds) that had slight though barely perceptible imperfections, and several of these also became heirlooms that still hang on my walls. My grandfather's health was not good and on his retirement we moved to a flat on the corner of Beach Road and Clifton Drive in St Annes-on-Sea (later Lytham St Annes). Sadly, after a few years my grandfather died of a heart condition but my grandmother, I'm pleased to recall, lived until she was ninety-four. So from the age of about 8 or 9 I was brought up by two doughty ladies to whom I am deeply indebted for their unfailing love and care and for ensuring that I had every opportunity to make the most of myself.

Before we left Trentham I had been at Miss Sworn's preparatory school in Longton and my mother was so impressed with the quality of the schooling there that after the move she arranged for me to be a boarder. Quite often at the beginning of term I was put on a train at St Annes or Blackpool in the charge of the guard who looked after me on the train and ensured that I was delivered at Stoke to one of the helpful collectors that had been assigned to get me to the school. I doubt if anything like that happens today.

When at the age of 9 I reached the end of preparatory schooling my mother transferred me to Arnold Junior School, a private school in

South Shore, Blackpool. I don't remember much of my first two years there but by the time I had reached the top form aged about 12 I first became aware that I had promising mental ability by coming top in end of term examinations. My other abiding memory of those days is that during the summer term a fellow pupil, Peter Will, and I were elected to captain two cricket teams, selected from the rest of the form, to play against each other. A coin was tossed to decide who had first pick. The team of the one winning the toss invariably won the match. Why was that? Because in the form was a young lad called Tom Graveney, whose skills even at that early age were far superior to those of the rest of us; so he was inevitably the first pick. Tom and his elder brother Ken and younger brother Maurice had moved into the area prior to the outbreak of war, though after only about a year or two were relocated, if memory serves, back to their native Gloucestershire. In those early days Tom was a useful bowler as well as an outstanding batsman. I have additional cause to remember him, though I doubt he would remember me, because in one match on a poor wicket he bowled a ball which popped and hit me in the eye. This rapidly closed, ensuring to my satisfaction that I got three days off school. However I'm afraid the downside of the incident was that always thereafter I had difficulty in suppressing a tendency to flinch when facing fast bowling. Maybe if we'd had helmets in those days I would have been more comfortable.

The only other injury I suffered from cricket was incurred some years later when bowling on an improvised pitch not far from the beach in St Annes in a game with my local pals. I dragged my foot in such a way that I tweaked the cartilage in my right knee resulting in synovitis ('water on the knee'). This left me hobbling for a week or two, ensuring that in visits to the Tower Ballroom in Blackpool to listen to Ted Heath and his band I was kept off the dance floor. This actually pleased me because I wasn't into dancing in those days.

Before that event, which historically is somewhat out of context, I had moved from the Junior to the Senior Arnold School, which could probably reasonably be described as having the status of a minor public school. The headmaster, Mr F W Holdgate, had a son, Martin, who was at the school but, being a couple of years younger than I, was in a form two numbers below that of mine. As a result I didn't see much of Martin at school and we didn't meet after I left school until nearly 30 years afterwards; but more of that later.

I progressed through school academically reasonably well and smoothly though I was invariably beaten out of first place in the exams by Pat Bradshaw, who like me later went on to Cambridge. On the non-academic side I got involved in all the three major sports that the school played, cricket, hockey and rugby, plus athletics and the Cadet Force. At this point I should reveal that, in keeping with my forbears, I am a minute specimen. I think my maximum height was barely touching 5ft 5in, and with the passing of years this has declined an inch or more. But I was fast and agile, with the result that I played in the major sports for all the school teams appropriate to my age (under fourteens, under fifteens, second and first XIs or XVs). I recall that in my first rugby match in the first XV against Blackpool Grammar School I scored a couple of tries playing at, I think, right centre threequarter and we won the match comfortably. However later in the season we suffered a humiliating 82-3 defeat at the hands of Kirkham Grammar School. They had a huge lad (named Jackson if I recall correctly) at centre who almost literally mowed us down and a fly-half who a few years later played for Lancashire. Actually our sports master, Bill Howarth, played regularly at fly-half for Lancashire and on at least one occasion was reserve for England. He was followed in that capacity by one of my sixth-form contemporaries, T K M (Mick) Kirby, who went up to Cambridge at the same time as I did though to a different college (Queens') and played splendidly for Cambridge in the Varsity matches. Sadly Mick died from cancer in his thirties.

But I suppose my greatest success in school sport was on the cricket field. Initially I bowled off-breaks, and because most of the groundsmen had been called-up the pitches were often so bad that I could almost literally turn the ball at right-angles. As a consequence in a match against St Joseph's College, a Catholic school in Blackpool, I took 8 wickets for 7 runs! I think it was in the same match that a very good friend Roy Marsh (of whom more later) was struck on the head by a bouncer. He recalls that as partial compensation while he was recovering in the pavilion they gave him an orange! Later, because on the bad pitches I could take wickets just by bowling as swiftly as I could to a good length, I gave up the off-breaks. In athletics the best I could do was third in the 100 yards and third in the mile.

Academically I can't recall much of note at school until I had reached the fifth form when the serious training for School Certificate began. In the final exams I gained 5 Distinctions and 4 Credits, though this again was surpassed by Pat Bradshaw who had 6 and 3 respectively (though well below the results achieved by later generations). We then went on to the upper sixth where we sat for Higher School Certificate. Pat gained a State Scholarship but I managed only a Lancashire County Major Scholarship. However my devoted mother scraped up enough to bridge the gap between the County Scholarship award and what was needed for me to go up to Cambridge.

The distance from our home in St Annes to school in Blackpool was about 5 miles. Initially I did the journey by bus to Squires Gate and then by tram the rest of the way. Fortunately the Blackpool trams at that time were among the best in the world and one of the tracks ran right past the school. However by the time I had reached about 14 or 15 I had acquired a bicycle and for the last 2 or 3 years of my school life I cycled to school and back every day. This was not particularly taxing except when an onshore wind was blowing across the sandy beach bordering the road sufficiently fiercely to produce a virtual sandstorm over the highway. I sometimes think that the amount of combing and scraping I did to remove sand from my hair was partially responsible for my premature baldness, though since my father had, I'm told, a bald patch at the back, genetic factors were probably more important.

Out of school in St Annes I was a member of a small gang of rather unlikely lads. I recall that one of our misdemeanours was to have what we called 'stone battles'. These consisted of dividing into teams and throwing stones, mainly beach pebbles, at one another to induce the retreat of our target combatants. Fortunately no one was seriously hurt, though there were certainly a number of minor injuries. One of the roads bordering where two of our local girlfriends lived was littered with stones and other debris – a situation which could only have been tolerated because it was war-time and those of the police who had not gone into the services had other preoccupations. Another of my personal misdemeanours resulted from my having acquired an air-rifle. On one occasion one of my school friends, known because of his girth as 'Fatty' Prestwich, held up a board for me to shoot at. Idiot that I was I decided to aim to hit just near Fatty's hand to give him a bit of a shock. Unfortunately my aim was bad and I hit him in the finger. The injury was not too serious, as it happened, but I suspect that if the same thing happened today it might have triggered a legal action.

Among our gang of boyhood school friends were Peter Jackson and Bryan Shaw. Peter was the son of a wealthy cotton-broker and went on from Arnold Junior School to Shrewsbury Public School. His mother and father were very generous to me, among other things taking us to shows in Blackpool and to dinner at the Pleasure Beach Casino. Peter came to see me once in Cambridge, mainly I think to complain about me taking out one of his girl friends when he was away. Subsequently, though not for this reason, I lost contact with him. I have, however, remained in touch with Bryan. After a distinguished career as a Captain in the Army he went into aeronautics, ultimately flying helicopters if memory serves.

Another feature of those early days was that we were very fortunate in Blackpool in getting many of the leading shows, often on trial as it were, before they transferred to London's West End. Also I recall seeing many leading performers, including George Formby, Arthur

Askey, Max Wall, Max Bygraves and Sally Gray. On one occasion at St Annes Cricket Club as a spectator I sat right behind Arthur Askey and remember being naively surprised that he was quiet and composed, quite unlike his stage persona (no 'Aiee thank you!'s).

Also in our gang was F C (Freddy) Hawksworth, who was at King Edward VII School in St Annes, nearly opposite the Royal Lytham Golf Club. Fred became one of the best amateur golfers in the country, winning, if I recall correctly, the Lytham Bowl, and numerous other prestigious trophies. His son John Hawksworth became a golf professional, playing on the European Tour. Then quite recently he has also featured as a commentator at certain UK tournaments alongside Peter Alliss and other notables, such as Alex Hay and Ken Brown. Mentioning Peter Alliss reminds me, albeit out of historical context, that about three years ago, when commentating he noted that the oldest pair of amateurs playing for an octogenarians' trophy were the Truckle brothers. As it happens the elder of the two, Bert Truckle, now still going strong at 97, is an old friend and fellow member of both Knebworth Golf Club and Stevenage PROBUS club, which I mention later.

My own experience in golf springs initially from my mother's interest in the game. When we moved to St Annes she joined St Annes Old Links, and although she was a modest long handicap performer I remember her coming home one day to announce that she had won the monthly medal; an event which resulted in her handicap being cut from 36 to 30. At the time the Old Links was considered to be about the equal of Royal Lytham, but during the war some holes were surrendered to make way for an expansion to Squires Gate Airport and somehow, after reconstitution, the course never seemed to quite secure its former status. I think I attempted without any training to play one round with my mother at the Old Links but at that time one was enough. However two or three years later I played several rounds with Fred Hawksworth and some of my other pals at the Green Drive Golf Club in Lytham. Although I enjoyed myself I performed poorly and since I was much more into other sports I didn't play again for about 10 years.

Other memories of those times include some splendid short holidays and days out with my half sisters, especially Zena and Margaret. They had each married Cambridge men, respectively John Carruthers and Ewart Akeroyd, both of whom read Chemistry contemporaneously at Emmanuel College and both gained their PhDs there. John joined the British Petroleum Company and had a very distinguished career in the oil industry. During and after the war he worked in Iran (then Persia) with the Anglo-Iranian Oil Company and subsequently became BP's top liaison man in Iran based in Teheran. Then after the Shah was deposed he returned to serve the few remaining years until his retirement as a senior executive near London.

Ewart Akeroyd, known by virtually everyone as 'Acky', obtained a Running Blue at Cambridge in addition to his academic accomplishments. After obtaining his Doctorate he did further postgraduate work at the Massachusetts Institute of Technology (MIT) in Boston USA before joining the Permutit Company back in the UK, the first member of the family to enter the water industry. Permutit specialized in the use of ion-exchange substances for water softening and deionization. At the time Acky joined the firm the ion-exchange materials were primarily naturally occurring inorganic zeolites, but before long synthetic organic resins were introduced with much greater and more specific exchange capacities. During the war Acky carried out pioneering work on the development of portable deionizing kits for converting seawater into water of potable quality for use by servicemen marooned in the sea. Subsequently he organized the introduction of factories in South Wales for producing synthetic exchange resins and went on to become Chairman and Managing Director of the Company.

Among numerous entertaining visits with these elder family members I particularly remember being taken by John and Zena to

Lords to watch the first day of Len Hutton's magnificent 364 not long before the outbreak of war.

In deciding which Cambridge College to apply for I was much influenced by our Headmaster F W Holdgate. He considered that being, at least in those days, a rather shy personality I ought to go to one of the smaller colleges, and we chose Sidney Sussex. I was glad that the choice didn't fall on Downing College, because I didn't want to be known as Downing from Downing. However I should have realized that wags among my fellow students would be apt to say, 'Are you Sidney from Downing or Downing from Sidney?'

When I went to Cambridge I always travelled there by rail after changing at Bletchley. It wasn't until about 40 years later that I realized that I had been so near the now famous code-breaking unit at Bletchley Park.

One of my fellow students was D G M (Gwilym) Roberts who was reading Engineering. Gwilym went on to have a very distinguished career in Consulting Engineering, becoming President of the Institution of Civil Engineers and being awarded a most well-merited CBE. He was a senior Partner in the firm of John Taylors, with whom the firm I subsequently joined, Binnie & Partners (see later), shared the premises of Artillery House, just off Victoria Street in London. Ultimately he was Chairman of Acer Group Limited.

I read Natural Sciences, which comprised Chemistry, Physics, Mineralogy and Maths. I played hockey and cricket for the College, being appointed Secretary and Vice-Captain of the cricket side in my second year. Plate 2 showing the 1946 XI reveals another of my many errors in that, although as Secretary I had arranged the photo, my name is inscribed as D L not A L Downing. Much against my personal preferences I was inveigled that year, because I was one of the two smallest members of the College, into coxing the Rowing Eight, an activity I needed like 'a hole in the head'. There followed two disasters. Towards the end of my first term I contrived to sink a sculler by hitting his small craft amidships with our racing eight. We were

2. Sidney Sussex College Cricket Team in 1946.

rowing downstream and I saw the sculler coming upstream. I yelled, 'Look ahead sculler', the approved warning, but he took no notice until he had almost reached us, when he appeared to sense our presence and turned broadside on in front of us. The by then unavoidable crash broke his craft in two. At the subsequent 'court of enquiry' chaired by the President of the University Boat Club it transpired that the sculler was deaf, thus accounting for his disregard of my warning shouts. On the other hand as a craft rowing upstream he was entitled to 'right of way'. The 'court' ruled that of the £35 required to provide a new craft (I think they called them whiffs in those days) our College had to pay 25%.

The second disaster occurred during the 'bump' races the following spring. We were bumped by the eight behind but in the process the prow of their boat flicked my rudder strings out of my hands. As a result we turned broadside on in front of a cavalcade of eights vigorously chasing one another and other eights moving upstream to take up positions for their turns in the events. It was a bit like those old movies with galleons crashing oars – complete chaos.

Following this debacle the College Boat Club released me from my obligations, their relief probably being as least as great as mine. This, however, was not the end of my aquatic mishaps, because during a holiday visit when my uncle gave me the tiller of his yacht on the River Crouch, I contrived to foul the vessel of the Commodore of the Royal Burnham Yacht Club, breaking off a pennant-bearing pole mounted at the stern. My uncle had to make our apologies and offer to pay for the damage, an incident which led to my being categorized as a 'Jonah'. This albeit warm-hearted stigma seemed to be confirmed when in a later sail on the Crouch we ran aground and had to abandon ship until it could be re-floated on the next tide in the early hours of the following morning.

I can't really claim that my rowing distractions at College had any significantly adverse effect on my poor performance in the following summer's Part I of the Natural Sciences Tripos examinations. The fact is that over the years, even before School Certificate examinations, I had fallen into the bad habit of coasting along, giving sport and other recreations almost as much attention as my studies, until just before the exams and then readying myself for the exams with two or three weeks of intensive revision. Up to that point this had worked adequately but on this occasion I fell 'flat on my face' and managed only a Third. Unfortunately this meant at the time that I could not proceed on to do Part II of the Tripos. I was awarded a Third Class Honours Degree but this merely had a status similar to that of an ordinary Pass Degree. As it turned out this was not sufficient to gain entrance to the higher ranks of the Scientific Civil Service for which an Upper Second in Part II was the minimum requirement.

CHAPTER 2

1946-50

AFTER LEAVING College I was placed on the Technical and Scientific Register and in some ways luckily instead of being called-up for National Service was required to get a job in science or other technology. My first interview was with a senior executive of the Mars company, who after regaling me with a glowing account of the company's activities during the War concluded with a triumphant, 'And we have just re-introduced Maltesers!' The salary offered seemed quite attractive but before making a decision I wanted to attend another interview that had been scheduled. This was one with senior members from several Government Research Stations. They outlined the work of their respective establishments but the one account that really fired my enthusiasm was from the Assistant Director of DSIR's Water Pollution Research Laboratory (WPRL) (Mr A E J Pettet). He mentioned, inter alia, the many opportunities there were to study at first hand the impact of pollution on natural waters, including rivers, estuaries, coastal waters and lakes. This combined with a fascination I had long had with water and its properties plus my (half) brother-in-law's involvement in the water industry persuaded me that a post at WPRL was just what I wanted. Thus I joined the Laboratory as an Assistant Experimental Officer at an annual salary of £253, well below that offered by Mars. The Director of the Laboratory was Dr B A Southgate, invariably called Bill (though not to his face) by his underlings, though his Christian name was actually Bernard. He was an excellent director and as it happened had a very helpful influence on my career. He died over 20 years ago at the age of 70.

My first assignment at the Laboratory was to investigate whether

13

passage of water through a device called an Aquastat caused any change in the water's composition. The Aquastat was essentially a metal tube round which was wrapped an electric cable through which current was passed, thus creating a magnetic field within the tube. The device was said to eliminate the formation of scale on heated surfaces through or into which the 'treated' water was passed. I could not detect any changes in quality but it soon became clear that in some cases the device worked and in others it didn't. The successful applications resulted essentially from the fact that any scale formed was easily dislodged soft aragonite instead of firmly adherent calcite (a different crystalline form of calcium carbonate). What was not clear then, and indeed as I mention later is still a trifle obscure, was the exact conditions needed to ensure preferential formation of aragonite.

After just a few months I was sent off to Wales with a colleague, Mr G F (George) Lowden, to join a team from the Atomic Energy Research Laboratory at Harwell who were investigating the suitability of water from various areas for cooling the planned first generation of nuclear reactors. Our job was simply to analyse the water drawn from Lake Trawsfynydd that was passing to a conventional power station at Penrhyndeudraeth. George and I spent that awful winter of 1946-7 in digs at Portmadog. We were taken to and from the site in the grounds of the power station each day by Humber 4x4 'battle wagons', former military vehicles. The weather and drifting snow were at times so bad that we had to cut our way through the drifts with shovels. At the weekends George and I spent a good deal of time huddled by the fire playing chess. The snow-clad scenery was magnificent. One didn't have to go far to see Snowdon in the distance; and on one of our occasional forays we went to Portmeirion to see the then avant-garde original developments which subsequently were expanded into the impressive facilities which many people will have seen as part of the backdrop for the TV serial, *The Prisoner.*

I was not privy to details of the Harwell team's investigations which broadly I believe were concerned with the extent to which the water might cause scaling and possibly corrosion of metals to be used in the reactor cooling circuits. By the spring sufficient information had been gathered and I was sent back to the Laboratory in Watford. I recall journeying through some of the worst flooding encountered in the area following upon the thaw.

I had not been back in the Watford Lab for very long before I was then seconded to the Fisheries Research Laboratory in Lowestoft to join a team that had been set up to investigate the possible impact on fisheries in the Irish Sea of discharges of effluent from the new nuclear facilities at Sellafield. I received some basic training in radiochemical analysis at Harwell and then became involved in measuring the uptake of radioiodine I^{131} and radiostrontium Sr^{89} and Sr^{90} (three of the most dangerous and prolific products of nuclear fission) by fish maintained in aquaria. We worked in a former radar trailer converted into a rather primitive laboratory and a small building at the end of Hamilton Dock. One of my co-workers was a biologist, Florence (Flo) Ryle, the sister of Martin Ryle the radio-astronomer (who was later knighted and became Astronomer Royal); another was Tom Davies, a physicist. Our boss was a lively character, built on the same scale as me, Freddy Morgan. Both Flo and Tom were Scientific Officers and thus my superiors, but in the nicest possible way engendered feelings in me that I needed to improve my status.

I lived in digs at the home of Tom Palmer, a clerical officer at the MAFF Lab, whose wife was an Olympic diver. I had a happy time with them, though at one stage I contracted chickenpox rather severely and had to spend a fortnight in bed. I played hockey and cricket for local teams and had one or two brief flirtations with local girls with whom I had played mixed hockey.

After about a year, by which time the likely rates of uptake of radioisotopes by fish had been brought into focus, I asked for and was granted a transfer to the Laboratory of the Government Chemist in London. This was facilitated by Dr Southgate who knew Dr Longwell, a senior member of the Laboratory of the Government Chemist and head of the Government Chemist's water department. The move allowed me to take up a place I had applied for at Birkbeck College to study part-time (essentially in the evening and weekends) for a Special Honours Chemistry Degree. My objective was to obtain at least a higher second (2i), which would give me much better job prospects, including the minimum requirement for entry into the Scientific Officer grade in the Scientific Civil Service.

Partly because I had moved south my mother and grandmother did likewise, buying a small house in Old Lodge Lane in Purley, Surrey. Subsequently they moved to a flat in Russell Hill, Purley, essentially because this was almost next door to the property of one on my mother's old friends, who had moved into the district and had known her when my father was alive. I lived with my folks, while working at the Government Chemist's Laboratory, travelling by train to London every morning and returning after my part-time evening classes to get home most nights at about 10 p.m. In many ways this must have been quite taxing, though I didn't really notice this much at the time.

In the Government Chemist's employ I was stationed not in their main premises in the Strand but as expected in the water department located in a former, but subsequently modified, workhouse in Endell Street. My job was essentially water analysis of samples coming in from various official sources all over the country. At lunchtime in the summer with one or two colleagues I used to go to the Oasis Swimming Pool which backed on to the water department building. One abiding memory of that time is having on a couple of occasions the privilege of watching, at fairly close quarters, the late Diana Dors, when she was just a young starlet, displaying her charms at the pool side.

At Birkbeck College, because I had already a basic degree, I had to spend only two years of study before sitting for the Special Honours Chemistry exam. Despite the high workload I had a great time recreationally at Birkbeck, among other things playing hockey and cricket for the College. One of my fellow chemistry students was

Dick Ringwald, who was a Czech by birth and a very good amateur tennis player, who practised his skills at the Queen's Club. He it was who took me to Wimbledon to see stars such as Jaroslav Drobny (his fellow countryman), Frank Sedgman and Rod Laver. Much to my relief I obtained a 2i Honours Degree in the examinations and I think Dick had either a 2i or a 1st. Dick went on to become Managing Director of a major chemical company. I had decided to resign from the Government Laboratory just before the Finals in order to have my usual period of intensive revision, which fortunately paid off on this occasion. Slightly to my surprise Dr Southgate at WPRL had learned of my 2i (possibly by his contact with Dr Longwell) and he telephoned me to say that he could offer me a post as a temporary Scientific Officer at the Watford Laboratory. From my previous experience this appealed to me greatly and I accepted immediately.

DSIR – 1950-54

When I returned to the Laboratory it was not long before I was drafted into a Radiochemical Section, housed in new laboratories at the Building Research Station (another DSIR organization) in Garston on the outskirts of Watford. This was headed by Mr G E (George) Eden with whom I was a colleague for about 40 years and have been a friend with him and his dear wife Daphne up to this day.

The Radiochemical Section had a very interesting assignment to examine the fate of nuclear fission products in conventional water and sewage treatment processes in the event of atomic explosions occurring in UK. As had been the case in the work with MAFF at Lowestoft interest centred principally on the fate of radiostrontium and radioiodine. Both passed through conventional processes either wholly or partially, except in the case of water treatment by ion-exchange softening when virtually all of the strontium was eliminated. However almost total removal of radioiodine was achieved during treatment of water by the conventional process of chemical coagulation settlement and rapid sand filtration by the addition of a minute quantity of silver nitrate, which precipitated the iodine as silver iodide.

My chief George Eden was kind enough to include me as a co-author of a paper recounting our observations regarding radioiodine in the *Journal of the Institution of Water Engineers* and as senior co-author of one concerning radiostrontium in the same journal – my first two involvements in publications.

While working at Garston one of our colleagues was a young lady zoologist called Kathleen Frost. Kathy was investigating the effects of pollution on freshwater fish. We started to date and in 1952 we were married. Roy Marsh was my best man. Kath and I have lived happily together ever since. I propose not to detail the events of our relationship because I regard these matters as private and sacred. Let it suffice for me to record that I consider myself extraordinarily fortunate to have been blessed with such a wonderful partner and later in 1957 with our beloved daughter Gillian.

Not long before our marriage I had bought, for £200, my first car, a 1936 BSA Scout, a four-wheel open-top sports car rather like the MGs of the time. The car had been laid up during the War and as I soon discovered was not in particularly good order. Its idiosyncrasies led me to perpetrate almost as many debacles as I had had with boats. The trouble was that the main bearings started to leak oil which settled on the transmission-brake in the centre of the front axle. The first time this happened, owing to the brake failing, I ran into the back of an army lorry. This didn't appear to damage the lorry but put a huge dent in my offside wing. Despite having to replace the main bearings at intervals of less than a year Kath and I drove up from Watford to Leyland to visit her family on several occasions. Kath's father, George Edward Frost, had been a Regimental Sergeant Major in the 5th Regiment of the Royal Artillery and in his service abroad had been awarded the Military Medal. Kath's brother, Edward, began his career in the Army but moved on into electronics, eventually setting up his own successful business in USA. I recall that on the evening of one

3. The Water Pollution Research Laboratory at Stevenage.

return journey from Leyland, which had taken the best part of a day, I had the frightening experience of momentarily nodding off at the wheel, when driving up the hill on the way through Knebworth. Fortunately the veering into the kerb jolted me awake in time to avoid damage and certainly taught me a lesson. I think that my last embarrassment occurred in Watford when I had parked the car in the late morning in one of a pair of parallel side roads which unknown to me at the time had almost identical parking areas. After doing some shopping I came back to the other road to find the car apparently gone. I dashed round to the Police Station, which as it happened was close nearby, and within a few minutes a couple of squad cars roared off to look for my supposedly stolen vehicle. After about 10 minutes they came back to me and a sergeant got out and said, 'Which pub did you have lunch in, Sir?' Of course they had found my car in the parallel road. Not long after, Kath managed to sell the car for me for £95, and we then bought an altogether better vehicle, a bull-nosed

4. Dr B A Southgate CBE at the entrance to WPRL.

Morris 8. This served us well for several years; and suffice it to record that our subsequent motoring experiences have been largely uneventful.

I think around the end of 1953 we received news that a new purpose-built laboratory was to be located in the developing New Town of Stevenage and we moved there in 1954. Plate 3 shows a picture of the Laboratory; and Plate 4 Dr Southgate in front of its entrance.

CHAPTER 3

WPRL Stevenage – The First Six Years: 1954-59

I THINK ONE OF the things I should be grateful for in this phase of my experience and indeed in subsequent phases is epitomized by the old adage 'a man who never made a mistake never made anything' – because I certainly made several more errors. My embarrassment has been only marginally reduced by the feeling that some of them became obvious only with the benefit of hindsight, to some extent perhaps inevitable when one is attempting to break new ground; but more importantly and luckily that none involved significant errors in full-scale practice or indeed so far as I am aware embarrassment to anyone other than myself.

At the beginning of the period which coincided with the move of the Laboratory to Stevenage I was switched from radiochemical work to lead a small team investigating factors affecting the rate of transfer of oxygen from air to water. In this team was a splendid colleague, G A (Geoff) Truesdale. Kath and I became good friends with Geoff and his charming wife Beryl and have remained so ever since. Among his many accomplishments Geoff became President of the Institute of Water Pollution Control (IWPC) in 1979, (the year before I did as I mention later) and then President of the Institution of Water and Environmental Management (IWEM) (later CIWEM), the body that evolved from IWPC; subsequently he was awarded a well-deserved OBE.

The interest in oxygen transfer at the air-water interface arose of course because this transfer is normally the main means whereby the dissolved oxygen removed in natural waters by biological

21

oxidation of organic and other oxidizable wastes released to them is replenished.

Almost immediately in our work on this topic Geoff Truesdale and I encountered a problem in that our measured concentrations of dissolved oxygen (DO) in water in equilibrium with the air (i.e. the saturation concentrations (C_s)) were always lower than the then apparently most reliable of the various published figures, those quoted in the American Public Health Association (APHA) *Standard Methods*.

We reported these findings in a letter to *Nature* and they became a subject of mild controversy. With the assistance of George Lowden we also made measurements exhibiting similar differences in seawater and published these in the *Journal of Applied Chemistry*. The differences of our values from the APHA figures varied with temperature but were greatest at low temperatures, when they were around 4%. We were concerned about this because rates of absorption (oxygen-transfer rates) were proportional to the oxygen deficit, the difference between the C_s values and the existing DO, and were evaluated from the slope of lines obtained by plotting natural logarithms of the deficits against time. Thus any error in the C_s could produce error in the estimated transfer rates. Although such errors would be small, provided that measurements of changes in DO were restricted to concentrations well below the C_s values, we decided to pursue the matter. The method of measuring DO we were using was a modified version of the conventional Winkler chemical method in which in effect the DO is converted into iodine which is then titrated. To cut a long and involved story short another colleague (Ian Hart) and I eventually found that in our method there could be a tiny loss of iodine to the atmosphere. Although the iodine losses that we measured were not enough to account for the whole of the differences between our method and the APHA values, and it was not clear why these differences were higher at low rather than at high temperatures, when the reverse might have been expected, we took a pragmatic decision at that point to continue using our method of analysis and our C_s values. This was partly because use of gasometric procedures would have been impracticable but essentially because by using the C_s values obtained by our method in conjunction with DO concentrations obtained by the same method the errors in estimating transfer rates would be negligible. A wealth of evidence obtained subsequently, some of which I mention later, showed that this assumption was sound. Subsequently another of our colleagues, Dr H A C (Harry) Montgomery, produced a definitive set of saturation values obtained by a gasometric procedure.

Having decided on the aforementioned course of action we then went on with the help of many colleagues to investigate the effect of all those variables that we could conceive of as having an influence on oxygen transfer (re-aeration) into natural waters. We made measurements in a variety of laboratory vessels, in a wave tank at a Docks and Inland Waterways laboratory and in natural waters and our colleagues did many more tests in flowing water and at weirs. The degree of agitation of the water surface and the extent of its contamination were as expected the two most important factors. All contaminants having surface-active properties (for example grease, oils, soaps, and synthetic detergents) reduced the rate of transfer considerably. The extent of the reduction depended on the original 'cleanliness' of the surface but could be as much as 60%. At around the time new synthetic detergents had been introduced which rapidly eroded the market for soaps and many of the original detergents were resistant to biological breakdown. In one of the papers I published reporting these effects a co-author was Mr A M (Alan) Bruce with whom I meet quite frequently these days, being fellow members of Stevenage PROBUS Club (see later).

However at this point I cannot proceed without reference to the profoundly important, 'ground-breaking' work that my colleagues, especially W S (Bill) Preddy and the late A L H (Hugh) Gameson did with the excellent guidance of the then Director 'Bill' Southgate to develop the first most comprehensive and thoroughly validated mathematical model for forecasting the effects of pollution on water quality and temperature in an estuary, that of the Thames. At the time about 20 to 30 km of the central reaches of the Estuary were habitually devoid of DO and hydrogen sulphide was being liberated to air from this thoroughly squalid anaerobic zone. The model enabled the best means of rectifying the problem and the associated allocation of the massive expenditure that this involved. Subsequently the model has provided an excellent tool for management of the Estuary by Thames Water and indeed is still the most thoroughly validated estuary model in existence.

Apart from my admiration of the work my colleagues did, which of course is inevitably among my memories, I mention the matter because I had a marginal involvement, albeit small, in the work at the time and later went on to develop a couple of features which I hope augmented the progress made.

One minor example of this is that our work on the effects of synthetic detergents helped to underpin the conclusions reached by our colleagues working on the Thames investigations that introduction of detergents was responsible for a reduction of about 20% in the rate of solution of atmospheric oxygen into the Estuary and thus to an appreciable worsening of the anaerobic conditions in the central reaches.

In parallel with the work on oxygen transfer I also had a brief involvement in a study of heat transfer in natural waters. One of the stimuli for this work was the fact that the temperature of water in a number of the UK's main rivers and estuaries was considerably elevated by release of cooling waters, especially from major power stations. To gain a knowledge of the effects of such releases on temperature distributions and on fish population was thus important. Accordingly an investigation was set in train and supervised by a Government Working Party. This resulted in Mr (now Dr) J S (John) Alabaster and myself carrying out a study using a labyrinthine channel constructed in the base of a disused cooling tower, from which the superstructure had been removed, at the former Grove Road Power Station at St John's Wood, London. At the time John was a member of the scientific staff of the Ministry of Agriculture Fisheries and Food (MAFF) though a few years later we were fortunate to have him join us at WPRL as a Division Head. My role was simply to measure and interpret rates of cooling of water flowing through the channels under various conditions. Basically these confirmed our expectations that rate of decline of temperature behaved approximately in line with Newton's Law of Cooling whereby the rate was proportional to the difference (the excess) between the existing temperature of the water and an equilibrium value which could be assumed with sufficient accuracy to be the wet-bulb temperature of the air. Our findings, mainly centred on the effects on fish, were reported in a joint paper (with John as the senior author) published by MAFF as part of their series of volumes on Fishery Investigations. In passing perhaps it will suffice to note that the findings of the study helped to underpin later investigations of the effect of heated discharges on the Thames Estuary and the effects of developments such as the Thames Barrier on the temperature of the Estuary.

As another by-product of the work on aeration systems for biological treatment plants I presented a paper in 1958 on 'Aeration in relation to water treatment' to a meeting of the Society for Water Treatment and Examination dealing with aspects of design of plants for removing (by air stripping) of unwanted contaminants such as methane, excess carbon dioxide, hydrogen cyanide, hydrogen sulphide and also the removal by oxidation of reactive constituents such as iron, manganese and sulphides. As it happened some speculations I made about rates of removal of methane in that paper became the foundation for estimates of removal rates I made about 30 years later in connection with the explosion at Abbeystead that I mention later.

It wasn't long after we had moved to Stevenage that when by chance we dropped into a local pub, the Lytton Arms, in nearby Old Knebworth, to our surprise we met an old school friend of mine,

Denis Welch. Denis was working in the accountancy department of the Stevenage Development Corporation and he and his dear wife, Barbara, who had also been a Blackpool resident whom I knew, were living, as it happened, not that far from us in the New Town. We got together quite often subsequently, sharing among other things an enthusiasm for golf, all of us being members of Knebworth G C. Both Denis and Barbara were rather better at the game than Kath and I, indeed Denis who was on the Committee of the Club soon became 'a near single-figures man' and eventually, though at another Club, got his handicap down to 5. Not many years passed, however, before as was normal in his line of work, he moved on to other venues, including Sheffield and eventually to Sleaford in Lincolnshire where he became Deputy County Borough Treasurer for the County of Kesteven. We kept in touch throughout and exchanged visits when the opportunity offered. Very sadly Barbara died recently from cancer and alongside Denis, their three accomplished sons and their families we miss her greatly.

My first overseas visit in a professional capacity took place in 1959 when I went to Liège to give a paper at one of the regular annual conferences organized by Professor E Leclerc at Centre Belge D'Etude et de Documentation des Eaux. The paper, published as a translation into French, was entitled 'Les effets des détergents synthétiques sur les processes d'aération' and looking at a reprint as I write I find myself 45 years later pleased with its account of the work we did in those early days. However, as usual, as will become apparent to anyone who reads much of this text, I remember nothing of the Conference itself. My only remaining memory is of being struck by the substantial accumulations of dust on the Liège streets. As it happens I have not been to Liège subsequently but I don't imagine that such accumulations would be tolerated now with Brussels EU HQ just round the corner.

For recreation I joined Knebworth Golf Club in 1956 and subsequently played there regularly. Playing in 1959 with Eddie

5. WPRL Cricket Team c. 1958.

Topham (with whom I still play quite often) we won the St John Hughes Trophy and with a lady member (Marjorie Clarke) the Tollafield Mixed Foursomes; and I lost the final of the Barker Cup. However, apart from an occasional monthly medal I have won nothing since. In the summer I also played cricket for a Laboratory side that, under Geoff Truesdale's captaincy, played local villages and teams from other Stevenage organizations. In one year either in the late 50s or early 60s we won the Stevenage Inter-Works League. I remember that in the final against George King Ltd I made a duck when batting but took 3 wickets when bowling. Kings had three men of West Indian stock in their batting line-up, each of whom looked capable of winning the match on his own. However I decided to bowl round the wicket to them and delivered a series of nippy near long-hops just outside the leg stump. Fortunately they all succumbed to the temptation to smash my deliveries to the leg boundary and 'holed-out' to square leg, where we had stationed one of our best fielders, Ralph

Game. He is shown in a photograph of the team (Plate 5). I'll have to admit that Ralph was not actually a member of the Lab. He was the son of a local garage owner but he was 'going steady' with the daughter of a member of the Lab's staff and had played regularly for us all season.

At around the same time Ken Melbourne and I made a brief study of factors affecting the performance of a method developed for applying a film-forming reagent, cetyl alcohol, on rate of evaporation of water from reservoirs. This is not a matter of much consequence in the UK but can be of considerable significance in hot countries. We found that performance was dependent on several factors many of which substantially reduced the effectiveness of the method. I have lost track of subsequent developments though my impression is that the method has fallen into disuse.

CHAPTER 4

Stevenage – The Next Six Years: 1960-65

IN 1960 I WAS very fortunate to be allowed to make my first visit to the USA comprising a $3^{1}/_{2}$-week tour of research establishments working on problems with features similar to those on which we were engaged at WPRL. At the start of the visit I had the first of three brief meetings (two of them much later) with the late Robert Maxwell. At the time he was the Chairman of Pergamon Press, who were instrumental in promoting the early International Conferences of the IAWPR and, of course, published their Proceedings. I cannot for the life of me now remember why but I had to collect from him about 300 US$ to cover my expenses during the tour. I remember asking him if I could have the money as some form of banker's draft, since I didn't fancy carrying around what to me in those days was a substantial sum. He brushed aside my concerns and insisted I take cash. When Pergamon Press were helping to foster the first of the IAWPR conferences, in London, Kath got co-opted with several other UK ladies to assist Maxwell's wife (a French lady) in formulating the Ladies' Programme. I know Kath found the lady almost as autocratic as I found her husband. However my two later meetings with him, both I think on the occasion of conferences, were much more relaxed.

I do not recall all my visits but they included New York (Manhattan College), Gainsville (University of Florida), Boston (MIT and Harvard), Durham (University of North Carolina), Universities at Urbana, Madison and Michigan and the Oceanographic Research Station at Woods Hole.

At Manhattan College I was able to have detailed discussions with Professor W W (Wes) Eckenfelder Jr and his co-worker Brother

Joseph McCabe whose joint research programme was very similar to the one I was pursuing at WPRL. I had many subsequent and felicitous meetings with Wes, as I note later.

Among non-technical features which particularly stick in my mind are staying with Professor Rupert Kountz and his wife in (I think) Pennsylvania and being presented by Rupert with a traditional Silver Dollar, which I still have; having a very pleasant time staying with Professor Jack Nesbitt and his charming wife; and meeting with Professor Gerry Rohlich and his very large family (about 9 or 10 children if memory serves) in Madison.

At Woods Hole I met John Kanwisher who was the inventor of the first so-called membrane electrode for measuring concentration of dissolved oxygen (DO). This electrode, which gave an almost instantaneous measure of DO in water in which it was immersed, was a highly convenient tool making possible automatic monitoring and control hitherto impossible using the conventional Winkler chemical method.

The tour finished in New York where I spent a night in the YMCA (surprisingly comfortable) and then the following day had a boat trip round Manhattan Island. I think it was either on this trip or a later one that I went out by boat to get a close look at the Statue of Liberty. Plate 6 is a snapshot I took looking back at the New York skyline.

I and my team, especially Mr A G (Arthur) Boon, then turned our attention to determination of the performances and factors governing performance of the large variety of aeration equipment used to supply oxygen to the biomass in the so-called Activated-Sludge Process (ASP) by this time the usually preferred method of secondary treatment of sewage from towns and cities and for many industrial effluent treatment plants. Because of the profound effect of synthetic detergents that we had found in our previous studies and the fact that virtually all sewages by this time contained substantial concentrations of these substances, we conducted a range of tests of aerator performance in the laboratory in water containing 5mg/l of alkyl

6. The New York skyline, seen from a boat in 1960.

benzene sulphonate (the principal component of most detergents excluding the non-ionic variety). As shown in our experiments this would accurately represent the rates in mixed liquors and avoided the necessity to take account of removal of DO by biological oxidation. In the case of the diffused-air system we underpinned this practice by collecting the air issuing from the aeration units in full-scale plants, determining its content of oxygen using paramagnetic oxygen analysers (which by then had come into the market) and showing that the results were in close accord with those obtained in laboratory tanks in water containing detergents. We also made increasing use of membrane electrodes for measurement of DO and the rate of its uptake by the biomass. This rate combined with the observed DO gave an indirect measurement of oxygen-transfer rates.

Without going into further detail about the wide range of tests we conducted, suffice it to record that we established the performance of all the main types of aeration system sufficiently well for design purposes. Perhaps not surprisingly we found that the best forms of all the devices gave similar oxygenation capacities per unit power and that no ideas for revolutionary means of improving on this came to light. One thing that did initially surprise us was that with aeration systems based on thrashing the water surface with rotating metal comb-like arrays (the originals being called Kessener brushes after the Dutch inventor) the presence of detergents actually increased oxygen transfer rates relative to those in water alone. This appeared to be the result of the increased interfacial area caused by the thrashing effect. However this finding did not alter the picture for full-scale practice. For a paper reporting some of our results that I gave to the Institution of Public Health Engineers in 1960, I was awarded the Institution's Bronze Medal for the best paper of that year. I must also add that around this time Kathy was co-author of several papers on the toxicity of various substances to fish and the sole author of one.

I next turned my attention to examining the scope for improving the design of the activated-sludge plants for biological treatment of wastewaters. In these plants the wastewater, usually after removal of settleable matter in primary sedimentation tanks, is mixed with a flocculent suspension of micro-organisms, the activated sludge, (or biomass in more modern terminology), and aerated, usually by diffusing bubbles of air into the mixed liquor or by mechanical agitation. Plate 7 which I refer to in more detail later shows three types of secondary treatment. The biomass brings about biological oxidation of the metabolizable constituents of the wastewater using the oxygen supplied by the aeration devices. The oxidizable matter destroyed is converted into more microbial biomass. After aeration the biomass is settled and most is recycled to the inlet of the aeration units. However to maintain a reasonably constant working level of biomass in the aeration units the excess biomass ('surplus sludge') produced from the oxidizable matter has to be continuously removed from the plant.

In domestic sewage and several types of industrial wastewater the

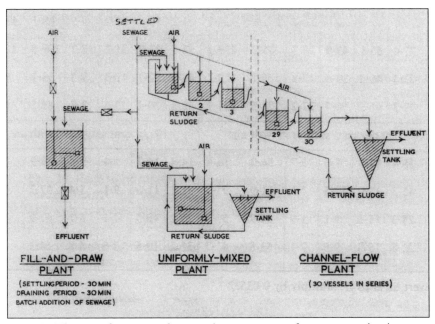

7. *Three configurations for secondary treatment of wastewaters by the Activated-Sludge Process.*

principal biologically oxidizable components are various types of organic matter and ammonia, and many plants were designed to achieve removal of both types of pollutant. In the UK several major works were required to produce final effluents complying with a so-called 10:10:10 standard, the figures representing the maximum limits on the content of 5-day biochemical oxygen demand (BOD), ammoniacal nitrogen, and suspended solids (figures which can be compared with around 500 mg/l, 50 mg/l and 500 mg/l in the case of raw domestic sewage). The removal of the organics giving rise to the BOD is brought about by a diverse mixture of heterotrophic bacteria; that of the ammonia by autotrophic nitrifying bacteria which oxidize the ammonia successively to nitrite and then nitrate; and that of the suspended solids by settlement after aeration sometimes followed by so-called tertiary treatment, most commonly by sand filtration. Unfortunately the conditions necessary to produce fully nitrified effluents complying with limits (such as 10 mg/l) on ammoniacal nitrogen were not well understood, with the result that several plants expected to achieve consistent nitrification did not do so.

In setting out to examine the reasons for poor nitrification in some plants I was eventually struck by the thought that, since the surplus sludge inevitably includes nitrifying bacteria, to maintain an effective level of these bacteria in the plant under constant conditions their percentage increase during aeration must be the same as the percentage increase in the concentration of the other components of the biomass. If it is below the latter percentage then the nitrifiers will be displaced out of the plant; if it is temporarily above this percentage then the content of nitifiers will decline until under constant operating conditions it becomes the same as that of the remainder of the biomass. Put another way this concept is simply that for a nitrifying population to develop in a plant they must initially grow at a greater rate than that at which they are taken away in the surplus sludge.

To convert this concept into design parameters my colleagues and I then had to determine the rate of growth of nitrifiers and that of surplus sludge. The rate of growth of nitifiers was measured reasonably straightforwardly by determining the change in the content of ammonia, nitrite and nitrate during aeration of batches of activated sludge. Such tests were conducted at various temperatures because we expected the rates to increase considerably with temperature as proved to be the case. Broadly the rates in a batch test increased exponentially, though as put forward by the French microbiologist, Professor J Monod, in his 1942 seminal paper, Recherches sur la Croissance des Cultures Bactériennes, there was a small effect of the concentration of substrate (in this case ammonia) at low levels. We produced a sidelight on this effect by analysing data that had been obtained previously by other colleagues working on the Thames Investigation, who had determined changes in the content of ammonia, nitrite and nitrate in batches of Thames water maintained at a series of constant temperatures. The concept evolved by Monod required that for the oxidation of ammonia to nitrite the growth-rate of the nitifiers should equal a product of a growth-rate constant (a specific growth-rate), their concentration, and a function of the concentration of ammonia and a saturation constant (referred to in enzyme kinetics as a Michaelis value). By fitting, by trial-and-error, integrated forms of this equation to the observations we obtained estimates of the three unknowns for a range of temperatures. Although, not surprisingly, the growth-rate constants were larger than those we determined from much other data for AS (Activated Sludge) plants the general pattern of the results underpinned and reinforced our concepts of the dynamics of nitrifier growth. The analysis of the Thames data was undertaken using the then relatively new Elliott 803 computer at Borehamwood. The lead in this work was taken by my colleague George Knowles who was much more advanced in computer technology than I and was senior co-author of a paper he, I, and another colleague, the late Mike Barrett, published about the work. He was also a co-author together with Dr Harry Painter of the first paper I presented on the kinetics of nitrification in the AS process. At the time, under George's guidance, I was just beginning to learn the techniques of programming, but regrettably I had only just got started when I was promoted; and from that day, I could almost say, to this I could always get someone to do the computations for me. Even now although I have two PCs sadly I remain something of a computer ignoramus, tending to rely on my daughter Gillian's assistance.

Another colleague, Adrian Hopwood (now the Reverend Hon Chaplain of the Worshipful Company of Water Conservators – see later), and I determined the relationships between rate of growth of biomass (sludge production) and operating conditions in laboratory-scale plants. We summarized the results by a somewhat unwieldy form of equation that I devised and which unsurprisingly has not been adopted by subsequent researchers. However there has been reasonably good agreement between the results predicted by their formulae and ours. In fact so far as I am aware the only divergent findings published have been some obtained from the main AS plant at Davyhulme Manchester by an old friend, Henry Tench. The reason for this has not been explained though my personal speculation is that it may somehow result from the sizeable component of industrial effluent in the Manchester sewage; a feature reflected by the rhododendron colour of the foam on the aeration units at that works. Combination of the relationships governing the growth-rate of nitrifiers and that of surplus sludge then gave us a complete definition of the conditions necessary to achieve nitrification in plants treating domestic sewage.

Two additional facets had to be taken into account before the picture was complete, as shown by our work and that of many others. One was that for nitrification to occur at maximum rate the concentration of dissolved oxygen (DO) had to be maintained above about 0.5 mg/l (roughly about 5 percent of the saturation concentration in water in equilibrium with the air). If DO fell appreciably below this level nitrification ceased. The second was that our studies identified a range of substances that were specific inhibitors of nitrifying bacteria. Such substances were not present in domestic sewage but could be found in some industrial wastewaters. From these premises we were able for the first time to establish the conditions and plant designs necessary to achieve nitrification and meet standards limiting the content of ammonia in effluents. Some of the practical implications can be illustrated by reference to the reasons why nitrification was not being achieved in many plants. Firstly, as was not appreciated before our study was undertaken, the concentration of biomass maintained in these units was not high enough to ensure that the fractional rate of increase in concentration of nitrifiers was greater than that of the biomass (the reciprocal of sludge age); secondly although in many cases this condition was satisfied in warm weather, because of the substantial effect of temperature on the growth rate of nitrifiers, it was not satisfied in winter conditions; thirdly, and perhaps most obviously, the aeration provided was insufficient to maintain DO in the mixed liquor on the aeration units above the minimum level of about 0.5 mg/l; and fourthly, nitrification was suppressed by the presence of specific inhibitors derived from industrial sources.

An interesting example of this last feature occurred when nitrification suddenly ceased at the Rye Meads treatment plant (in the Lee Valley) which received sewage from Stevenage, Welwyn Garden City and several other towns in the region. This cessation was serious because the Rye Meads plant was legally required to produce effluent complying with a limit of 10 mg/l on content of ammoniacal nitrogen. To investigate the matter at WPRL we took samples of the sewage from various parts of the drainage system and aerated them in admixture with a nitrifying activated-sludge. As it turned out the only samples that suppressed nitrification were of sewage draining from Welwyn Garden City. Further examination revealed that the problem was caused by release of a small concentration of thiourea, an exceptionally powerful inhibitor, from an ICI factory in the town. A useful by-product of the work was the development of a new technique by Harry Montgomery for measuring the separate contributions of nitrification and bio-oxidation of carbonaceous matter in the 5-day BOD test, the conventional means of assessing the potential oxygen demand of wastewaters. This simply involved addition of a small concentration of alkyl thiourea to suppress nitrification in one sample and then determining the total BOD in an 'unsuppressed' sample.

Another important outcome of the work evolved from our observations that the nitrogen content of the effluents from the plants, when in nitrifying mode, was invariably well below that in the influent. This was clearly due to the occurrence of denitrification a well known phenomenon caused by the bacterial reduction of nitrate and nitrite under so-called anoxic conditions. These occurred when dissolved oxygen in the mixed liquor was reduced to low levels in the sedimentation tanks. Although the phenomenon was well known it had not been realized that the removal of nitrogen could be as large as those experienced in our experiments. This finding was in effect a forerunner of the subsequent development of the process for nitrogen removal to meet standards adopted a few years subsequently imposing limits on nitrogen content and also that of phosphorus, principally to avoid development in receiving waters of troublesome growths of algae, which utilize these nutrients for their growth (or in the case of a few nitrogen-fixing species just the phosphorus). Because, at the time of our work, there was no demand for imposition of such standards in UK we did not pursue this aspect and much of the initial research to evolve suitable designs was carried out abroad.

In passing I should just add that removal of phosphorus by chemical precipitation of phosphate was a straightforward possibility and in many circumstances would alone have sufficed to eliminate excessive algal growth, though it would have increased sludge production to some extent.

In looking back to this period I think it fair to claim that what we did had groundbreaking significance for evolution of biological treatment of wastewaters. Certainly that view appears to be supported by my being awarded the Dunbar Gold Medal of the European Water Association in 1975 (see later), the citation for which refers to the work as being a 'crucial contribution'.

An interesting facet that I had noted in our various experiments was that the biomass in our fill-and-draw plants settled very much better than that in our other plants, especially those which had a single uniformly mixed aeration unit. This suggested that biomass settleability might be dependent on the degree of longitudinal mixing in the aeration units because the regime applied to the biomass in fill-and-draw plants could be regarded as typifying that which would occur in a plant in which the biomass moved through the aeration units with ideal so-called 'piston flow' (i.e. without any longitudinal mixing). Accordingly I arranged for the matter to be investigated further using three laboratory-scale plants (Plate 7, mentioned earlier), in which in one the aeration unit was operated in fill-and-draw mode, in another it was uniformly mixed and in the third it was composed of 30 uniformly mixed chambers in series (actually far more than the number of baffled compartments in any full-scale plants as far as I am aware). The tests were conducted at a series of different biomass loadings (mass of BOD applied per unit of biomass). The results (published in our 1966 Annual Report) showed that except in one case the biomass settleability (as judged by sludge-volume index) in the thirty-stage and fill-and-draw plants was always better than in the uniformly mixed plant. However the difference at low biomass loadings typical of those adopted in plants designed to achieve high quality effluents (especially those required to achieve nitrification) was small and almost certainly not of practical significance. The effect of the biomass loading, however, was much more important, the settleability of the biomass in the uniformly-mixed plant being at high loadings much poorer than that in the others, except in the one case already mentioned, and in all cases sludge-volume indices were much higher than at low loadings. A reservation that perhaps should be made was that the experiments were conducted at constant flow, rather than with the daily variations typical in full-scale plants and with purely domestic sewage, though I doubt whether these factors would have had appreciable influence. One other aspect though only qualitatively observed was that the biomass in the fill-and-draw plant appeared much more granular than in the others and appeared to coagulate fines less well. Later, when in private practice, these results influenced my thinking about the design of a full-scale plant (see later).

Among other events generating memories in this period was being assigned in 1964 to take part in what I understood was a revival of wartime meetings to exchange ideas between public and private sector individuals expected to proceed on to more important posts. The party comprised twelve from each sector and proceedings were conducted by a senior man from the CBI (I think his surname was Whitehead) and the historian Alan Bullock (later Lord Bullock who regrettably died just recently). We were accommodated at a notable building called the Node near Codicote in Hertfordshire and the format was that we worked in syndicates in the morning, had the afternoon off for leisure activities and then in the evening had lectures followed by discussions from notable public figures. These included Sir Edward Boyle, one of the Laing family (civil engineering contractors) and Richard (later Baron) Beeching who I recall looking rather gloomy following the abandonment of some of his plans to close various rail links. At one of the morning sessions under the supervision of Alan Bullock I had to chair a debate about the value of planning enquiries. We had gone through most of the allotted time and although a wide range of views was expressed we didn't appear to be reaching any useful conclusion. Finally I said something along the lines of that, 'In my opinion the value of planning enquiries is not that they necessarily guarantee good plans but that they minimize the chance of something important being overlooked.' 'That's the point,' said Alan Bullock with considerable emphasis, I suspect his relief being nearly as great as mine. We concluded shortly afterwards on that note with the approbation of fellow participants. In our recreational breaks I was able to take advantage of the fact that Knebworth Golf Club of which I was a member was only a few minutes' drive away. As a result I took three fellow participants on a couple of occasions to play the course. One other thing I recall is going ten-pin bowling in Stevenage fairly late one night with one of my fellow public service participants, who had learned during the course that he had been appointed British Ambassador to Laos and Cambodia. Regretfully all I can now add is that I think his surname was Warner.

Also in or around 1964 a Partner of a paper industry consulting firm, Cross & Bevan (C & B) from nearby Arlesey (as I mention later), came to the Laboratory asking if someone could assist them by advising on the likely consequences of release of effluent from a recently completed pulp and paper mill to the Sado estuary, south of

Lisbon in Portugal. The independent assessment was required because the Portuguese mill owners had omitted to get planning permission! Bill Southgate detailed me to do the job and accordingly I went to Lisbon to meet up with C & B's man and a party of Finns who had been involved in the design of the mill. There was of course no way in which an accurate assessment of effects could be obtained in a few days' visit. Such an assessment would have required development of a water quality model but the feeling was that based on for example our experiences in the Thames Investigation the Laboratory was probably better placed than any other organization to give a view on the matter. Fortunately the mill facilities included a state-of-the-art treatment plant and this coupled with such other information as I could glean about the Sado, which is quite a large estuary, I concluded that the discharge would probably not produce a significantly damaging effect. I gave this view to a senior Portuguese official and the 'green light' was given to the project. So far as I am aware over the years since then my view has proved adequately reliable. The Finnish cohort were obviously keen to keep me in the right frame of mind by arranging excellent wining, dining and entertainment in the evenings and on one day took me out to lunch in Estoril, where after eating some seafood that looked a little like black twigs my face came out in red blotches. This was initially somewhat alarming but after a while they subsided and eventually disappeared. I should perhaps just add that the entertainment didn't influence my judgement of the effects on water quality in this altogether memorable trip.

At around this time my boss (Dr Southgate) arranged for me to attend a Gordon Conference in New Hampton, New Hampshire, USA. These conferences were designed to provide a sort of 'think-tank' forum for researchers to exchange ideas about the current problems and their possible solutions, in the relevant field, water pollution control, of course, being that of the one I attended. Regretfully all I can remember of the technical proceedings is talking about the work in progress in the UK to replace the biologically non-degradable 'hard' components of synthetic detergents (alkyl benzene sulphonates) by 'soft' alternatives; and being quite gratified that this seemed to impress my largely American audience. Although the time of the conference was well before the 'fall' and the venue was north of Vermont I was struck by the remarkably attractive scenery of the area and made to feel at home by travelling through or near locations with English names, such as, in addition to Hampshire, Manchester and Worcester. This illusion was slightly dented on the occasion when in one of the recreation periods we played a round of golf at a local course. For the first and only time in my golfing experiences, when I went to play my ball, which was in the light rough, I found curled up beside it a yellow and green looking snake. Possibly it was a harmless grass snake but I advanced on the ball with club in hand in some trepidation. Fortunately as I began to address the ball the snake slithered off into the undergrowth – end of story.

Also in 1964 I was prompted by Dr Southgate to accept an invitation from Professor Mostertman of Delft University to give a course of lectures on treatment of industrial wastewaters at the International Institute for Hydraulic and Environmental Engineering at Delft. I believe this was the first year that Environmental Engineering was introduced to the curriculum which formerly had been devoted solely to hydraulics. Kath came with me and we stayed at the former Wilhelmina Hotel. I greatly enjoyed lecturing to students from a wide range of countries and we had a very pleasant time in the evenings looking round the old city and sampling its many excellent restaurants. Indeed we enjoyed our time so much that I accepted an invitation to repeat the excursion the following year and went on doing just that every year until 1994 (a total of 30 years). The visits afforded me welcome opportunities to meet with old friends in the same line of business particularly, in addition to Professor Mostertman, two meritorious pioneers in wastewater treatment, Professor J K Baars and Dr Pasveer, the latter being the inventor of the now widely used 'oxidation ditch' for small flows of domestic and industrial wastewater; also Willi von der Emde who went on to take a Professorial Chair in (I think) Vienna, Professor Caryl Morris of Harvard University and on one occasion his colleague there, Professor Werner Stumm.

After the first few years we decided there was more to do in our recreational periods in the Hague than in Delft and we stayed many times at the Park Hotel de Zalm in the Moelenstraat (not far from the grounds of the Royal Palace) and within walking distance of the splendid art gallery, the Mauritshuis. We invariably took the car from Harwich to the Hook, filled with the usual travel baggage, plus piles of lecture notes and slides and those vital articles, our golf clubs. Apart from sightseeing the car was very useful in getting me from the Hotel to the International Courses (and the golf courses) and back especially on the quite frequent occasions when I had to be ready to start my lectures at about 8.30 a.m. We played many rounds of golf in the early years at the Hague Country Club, which has a magnificent course in the dunes near the coast, and has often been the chosen venue for the Dutch Open (and I think other European PGA events). We were also frequent visitors to Scheveningen, a splendid seaside resort close to the Hague. We also played a few rounds in the last few years of my participation in the Courses at a recently opened new course at Delft though this was not in the same class as the Hague Country Club. Other events that particularly stick in my memory are visits to the gardens at the Keuchenhof, to the museums and art galleries in the Hague and Amsterdam, to the auctions of flowers and bulbs at the centre near Amsterdam and to the famous Delft pottery. Curiously we never got to the pottery during my period in the Courses but only finally in a trip with Stevenage PROBUS Club (see later) just a few years ago. I remember this especially because I decided to buy as a souvenir an attractive small plate depicting a pleasant rural scene. My enthusiasm for this was partly triggered by misreading the price tag and thinking that I had only to pay £40, whereas in fact the price turned out to be £400. Fortunately my credit card was accepted and I have never regretted the mistake; the plate now hangs in our dining room where I see it with pleasant nostalgia nearly every day. Another reminder of these times is shown in Plate 15, which is a picture of part of Amsterdam, painted by Kathy, who is in my view, and that of others who have seen her paintings, a pretty good amateur artist.

I think it must also have been in 1964 that I was first sounded out to ascertain whether or not I would be prepared to succeed Bill Southgate as Director when he retired. Having said that I would (albeit with some trepidation) I was then appointed to be Deputy Director pending the eventual promotion to the 'hot seat'.

Also in 1964, having become conscious that my work had moved more into the field of chemical engineering than of chemistry, I applied for Associate membership of the Institution of Chemical Engineers (I Chem E). I did so under a rule that permits applications from people aged over 35, who are not graduates in the subject, provided that they submit an acceptable thesis on a relevant topic. I wrote a thesis on means of introducing, by aeration, 100 tons per day of dissolved oxygen into the anaerobic zone in the middle reaches of the Thames Estuary. By chance I still have a copy of the thesis. Of course artificial aeration was not the best way of dealing with the polluted part of the Estuary, as I have mentioned earlier, but the object of the thesis was simply to demonstrate that one was conversant with the relevant chemical engineering concepts. Much to my pleasure my application was accepted and I went on in 1975 to become a Fellow of the Institution.

In the early sixties excellent work had been done by George Eden, Geoff Truesdale and other colleagues to assess the effects, on the composition of sewage and sewage effluents, of the replacement of the original 'hard' (i.e. non biologically degradable) anionic detergents (alkyl benzene sulphonates) by new 'soft' varieties. In 1965 George Knowles and I set out to use data obtained by this team to examine the kinetics of removal of the new types in laboratory-scale and continuous flow AS plants. Omitting detailed consideration of a slightly complex concept here, we envisaged that the new types on the market contained a mixture of mainly soft plus a fraction of hard components. We further assumed that depending on circumstances the detergent molecules were rapidly adsorbed on to the biomass (the AS) then the soft variety were rapidly desorbed to replace the concentration of soft components that were biologically degraded within the liquid phase. We then postulated that in a plant that had previously received only detergent-free sewage, either the existing heterotrophic bacteria became adapted through biochemical enzyme transformation so as to be able to degrade the soft detergents, or a small seed of organisms already with this capability grew and increased in concentration rather as we had demonstrated to occur with nitrifiers. In reporting our ideas we considered that the former mechanism was the more likely, though either concept would have led to similar conclusions. We then went on to make quite good, though by no means perfect, predictions of the residual content of detergent in the effluents from the laboratory plants operating under a range of conditions. As it happened one of my colleagues, Dr Gordon Jones, was quite sceptical about our enzyme adaptation hypothesis, preferring the growth of a bacterial species with the intrinsic capability to degrade detergents as the more likely mechanism. Looking back on the matter nearly 40 years later I remember at the time taking account of the fact that if a new detergent-degrading population developed then at equilibrium the fractional increase in its concentration in each aeration cycle would have to be equal to the fractional increase in the biomass concentration as a whole. When I calculated the implication of that at the time I recall obtaining a figure for the concentration of the detergent-degraders which seemed inconceivably high. When I do the calculation now I get a figure of around 100 to 150 mg/l, which in relation to the total biomass concentration of typically 3000 mg/l seems quite conceivable. I begin to wonder whether in rushing to complete the paper to meet a deadline for presentation at the Third IAWPR Conference in Munich in 1966 I made a stupid arithmetical error.

I cannot now recall the arguments that Gordon Jones put forward in support of the bacterial growth hypothesis, but I incline to the view that he was probably right. For all that so far as I am aware no one has subsequently isolated, cultured and identified the hypothetical detergent-degrading organism. Ironically the growth of a particular species of organism, would have indirectly provided further support if any were needed about our hypothesis for nitrification. An additional irony, though not necessarily prejudicial to the organism-growth hypothesis, is that more recent investigations into the content of the biomass in AS plants have indicated that only a small proportion of the heterotrophic organisms in a typical AS biomass are viable, the moribund populations functioning more as 'mixed-bags of enzymes'.

CHAPTER 5

1966-74

THEN AT THE age of 40 I was appointed Director, in succession to Dr Southgate, in the spring of 1966. At the same time I was promoted to Chief Scientific Office Grade B, being I understand the youngest in that Grade at the time throughout the Department. Two diverse consequences were associated with this. One was that I had to be 'Positively Vetted' by the security services; the other in contrast was that I received an invitation to be included in *Who's Who*. The first of these events provoked some ribald teasing, years later, by former school friends who had been quizzed by the intelligence services; the second may have been responsible for my being contacted by the Memoir Club?

Details of events at the Laboratory during my period as Director are comprehensively summarized in the *Annual Reports*, produced in the late autumn and published by HM Stationery Office at the beginning of the following year. Obviously I am biased but in my view these Reports, which in many ways were almost unique, were models of the way a Government Research Establishment should keep its 'customers' informed of what had been achieved with the public funds allocated. These Reports were substantial documents which took quite some effort to prepare. In their pre-1970 format, (roughly 21 by 14 cm) they extended to over 200 such pages that year; and in their subsequent A4 (21x29 cm) format up to 1973 they embraced around 130 pages. They were composed of individual contributions from Division and Section Heads, and edited by George Eden the Assistant Director. They also included a short foreword by the Department's Director-General of Research and a longer one by myself setting out

the salient features of the year's results and the reasons for the course
we had pursued. So far as I am aware very little or nothing like this is
done today and I can't help but think that the country is the poorer for
this. With all this already in print, although still in my memory, I see
no point in attempting any kind of comprehensive recapitulation here.

Very briefly the Laboratory's work was divided into about a dozen
main areas concerned with: coastal pollution; estuaries; freshwater
streams; effects of pollution on fish; aerobic biological treatment
processes (the AS process and percolating filters); sludge treatment;
sewage composition and properties; industrial wastes; microbiology;
methods of analysis; and instruments. Our programme also involved
some international studies for example to determine the scope for
advanced non-biological means of sewage treatment, enabling nutrient
removal and water reclamation (NATO); the scope for wider use of
incineration processes in sludge disposal (EEC); to identify the
'unknown' components of sewage effluent (EEC); and the influence
of eutrophication on algal growth in reservoirs (OECD). Just a very
few aspects of the work are illustrated in the photographs (Plates 8-11,
16 and 17). The one (Plate 10) showing the late Dr R S (Bob) Gale
evokes particularly poignant memories because having done much
meritorious work on improving the technology of dewatering of
sludges, Bob sadly developed multiple-sclerosis and died relatively
young.

In what now follows I deal mainly with those events in which I had
a close personal, as distinct from administrative, involvement but not
detailed in the *Annual Reports* together with a few sidelights on some of
the many things that were.

During my time as Director largely as a result of the great increase
in public awareness of environmental concerns our budget and staff
numbers increased by about 50 percent and the numbers of visitors to
the three Open Days that we held each year from around 1000 in 1965
to 5000 in 1973.

Although I had served on a few committees before becoming

8. Biological filters at the Laboratory.

Director, once I had done so the number of these increased dramatically, attendance at them taking a considerable proportion of my time. In due course I would probably have been able to delegate some of these duties but as I explain later 'due course' never came. To begin with in 1966 the Laboratory had a steering committee and 3 joint advisory committees with respectively the CBI, IWPC, and the Association of River Authorities, together with a Basic Research Committee and a Coastal Pollution Research Committee; later all but the last were amalgamated into a Central Advisory Committee.

Added to these were the Ministry of Housing and Local Government (MHLG) Technical Committee on Storm Overflows and the Disposal of Storm Sewage; the MHLG Technical Committee on the Disposal of Solid Toxic Wastes; the MHLG Water Quality Steering Committee, later the Department of the Environment's (DoE's) Water Quality Advisory Committee; the Natural Environment Research Council's Freshwater Sub-Committee; the

9. Study of the treatment of sewage by reverse-osmosis.

*10. Dr R S (Bob) Gale welcoming the German Federal Minister of Health to
the Laboratory's stand at a Munich Exhibition, 1969.*

11. Small-scale activated-sludge plants.

Council and Research Advisory Committees of the Water Research Association (later the Water Research Centre's Council) and of the Freshwater Biological Association; the CIRIA Hydraulics and Public Health Engineering Research Committee; the Society of Chemical Industry's Industrial Water and Effluents Group Committee (of which I was Chairman from 1969 to 1971); the UK National Committee of the International Association of Water Pollution Research (IAWPRC) and the CBI's Water and Effluents Panel. I also served on the Editorial Advisory Board of the *Effluent and Water Treatment Journal* and later on that of the *International Journal of Environmental Sciences* (Section B).

However I still found just about enough time to cope with my administrative role, and for a period to continue to take a close personal interest (too much I suspect some of my former colleagues would say) in the research in which I had formerly been directly engaged.

Most of these committees met in the south-east but two exceptions were those of the Freshwater Biological Association which naturally were held at the FBA laboratory at Ferry House, Windermere, and that of the Scottish branch of the CBI which held meetings with the Scottish River Purification Boards in Edinburgh. In both cases my practice was to go up by train the day before the meeting, stay overnight at a hotel and come back the following night by sleeper. Often on the evening before the sleeper departed I would go to the cinema but I've lost track of the number of films of which I never saw the last half hour because of having to dash for the train. My former chief 'Bill' Southgate told me that when he first went to the Scottish meetings the technical people had to sit behind the administrators and only speak when spoken to. Happily that had all passed by the time I inherited the commitment. The journeys to Ferry House were quite nostalgic because as a boy I used to go up to Windermere to 'camp out' on a boat owned by one of my school friends, Bryan Shaw's father.

Another of my involvements (already briefly mentioned) just before and during my time as Director was with the Society of Chemical Industry's Water and Effluents Group. Meetings were held about three or four times each year at the Society's elegant premises in Belgrave Square. I served as Chairman in the period 1969-71. After the meetings we used to repair to a nearby pub for lunch (and drinks). There were some notable industrial scientists among the Committee including Dr C J (Chris) Jackson and Gordon Lines (of the Distillers Company), Dr D H (David) Sharp and John Hewson (all regrettably now deceased).

In the first year of the period items of particular personal interest included the fact that the Laboratory demonstrated that a relatively simple method I had initiated for modelling vertically well-mixed estuaries, the so-called mixed-segment model, gave results nearly identical with those of the quantized mixing model used in the original Thames Investigation. This was pleasing because it paved the way for successful use of the method by myself and others for a number of other estuaries. I gave a paper including an account of the method to an Annual Meeting of the Association of River Authorities and the paper was published in the Association's *Yearbook* in 1967. At that meeting I remember slightly shocking some of my audience with an account of what the Laboratory had found when analysing the water in Stevenage's main swimming pool. The content of ammoniacal-nitrogen in the water was the equivalent of what would be formed from hydrolysis of urea in a release averaging between about 10 and 60ml per user. A mitigating factor of a kind was that the majority of users were often schoolchildren.

Also around this time I prepared a paper with Dr R W (Ron) Edwards, one of our Division Heads, on the effects of pollution on rivers, for an IWPC Annual Conference. Ron left the Laboratory a little later to take a professorial Chair at the University of Wales IST. His many distinctions included becoming, if memory serves, Deputy Chairman of Welsh Water and receiving a well-merited CBE.

I was author or co-author of four other papers in the same year. The necessity to communicate results in print continued on throughout my Directorship so that during the whole period I authored or co-authored some 30 publications. Most of these were for scientific or technical journals in the English language; but one, surprisingly perhaps, was an article for the *Financial Times*, one for the *New Civil Engineer* and five others for French (2), Dutch and German (2) journals. I have to admit right away that the French and German ones were translated from my English script by the Laboratory's Chief Librarian (Miss N Johnson) and her staff and I think the one for a Dutch journal was either translated by the journal's staff or printed in English. While on this subject I must also admit to using a somewhat similar 'dodge' to give an interview in French on French radio. A smart young French lady came to my office to discuss the interview. I told her that my French was minimal (a Distinction in School Certificate certainly did not raise me above that level) but as it happened I had just enlisted in a conversational class in Welwyn Garden City. So she gave me the questions she wanted answered in English. I took these to the tutor of the French class, said what I wanted to reply in English and then had this translated into French both audibly and in writing by the tutor. I then met with the French reporter the following day and gave the required interview. A month or two later I happened to meet some French professionals in the water industry who had heard the broadcast. 'How was it?' I said. 'Oh it was OK,' they said, 'but we knew you weren't French!'

In 1966 my memberships of the then Institute of Water Pollution Control was upgraded to Fellowship; and the same change also took place in 1968 with the then Institution of Public Health Engineers.

Around about this time I was elected a Fellow of the Royal Society of Arts and recall that when receiving my certificate also enjoying the same experience was the well-known actor Donald Sinden (though I doubt that he would remember me). About 20 years later I resigned because having so many other commitments I couldn't take part in many of the Society's functions.

Then in 1967 I applied for a DSc (Doctor of Science) from London University. Unlike a PhD which is usually the target end-product of three years' research at university following graduation, for a DSc one has to submit one's publications for review, usually by a Professor in the appropriate discipline, and whoever the Professor decides to co-opt to assist. I submitted 40 publications which included one or two that contained misconceptions that I mention later and another which, as I subsequently discovered, included an absurd, though fortunately having no practical significance, mathematical error (apparently also missed by whoever refereed the paper). However the 'positives' must have well outweighed the 'negatives' and I was delighted when my application was accepted and I was awarded a DSc in Biochemical Engineering.

Though I cannot remember the date, around this time I had my first television interview. This was conducted by the late Leonard Parkin and focussed on the environmental impact of coastal pollution from marine sewage outfalls. Under the guidance of a Coastal Pollution Research Committee, of which I was Secretary, the Laboratory had been conducting detailed investigations into the fate of pollutants released into the sea and the influence of important variables such as the depth of the outfall, its distance offshore, the degree of pre-treatment of the sewage before release and important environmental factors such as solar radiation intensity and tidal movement. The work had begun around 1962 and was still in progress in 1973, though by that time the essential information had been largely obtained. Broadly the study identified the design features required to prevent serious health hazards and visual evidence of pollution and to meet bacterial standards being introduced by the European Community for bathing beaches. At this time, although it was clear that minor ailments could follow simply from bathing, even in the cleanest of waters, there was uncertainty in some quarters about the possible extra extent of such ailments associated with bathing even in waters near apparently satisfactory outfalls. However encountering one of the hazards of TV interviews the programme ran out of time before I could mention this to qualify my assertion that based on a classical MRC Report there was no risk of serious health infections from bathing in waters in which there was no gross visible evidence of pollution.

This was the first of three interviews I have given in the UK. The second took place in the garden of my home. It was about some incident in the Home Counties but for the life of me I cannot now remember what. I can recall that whatever it was I considered that the responsible authorities would be able to deal with it without difficulty. The third interview was part of a documentary about some of the research activities at the Laboratory. Subsequently I have done seven interviews in various overseas locations but I deal with these elsewhere.

I attended quite a few international and national conferences usually in a quite active role as presenter of a paper or Chairman of one or more sessions and sometimes both.

After I had become Director Arthur Boon rounded off our work on aeration systems and in the process was able in effect to correct one of my mistakes. This had arisen from the fact that when interpreting data from the experiments that we had conducted to measure oxygen transfer rates in a tank simulating the configuration in full-scale ridge-and-furrow diffused-air plants, I had asserted that there was an effect of the depth of water aerated on the rate of oxygen transfer from the bubbles. It was perfectly obvious that in varying the depth of water in the tank we were also introducing a second variable, the volume of water per unit depth. However at the time I thought, stupidly as it turned out, that transfer rates would be highest at the moment of bubble formation and were so dominated by the 'resistance' at the air-water interface that, under the test conditions, variations with depth in the rate of transfer from below the interface through the bulk of the water would not be great enough to have a significant effect. I was also influenced by the results of another, relatively crude set of tests that we had made which with hindsight were probably liable to the same sort of error arising from having two variables instead of one.

However by around this time plant designers had begun to change from the ridge-and-furrow configuration to units with flat floors, which could more readily accommodate the additional diffusers needed to maintain DO at levels suitable for achieving nitrification. Arthur and another colleague (John Lister) had meanwhile set up another tank similar to the one we used originally except that it had a flat floor. In this, as readers may now expect, there was no significant variation in transfer rates with depth. They then inserted panels in effect to recreate the ridge-and-furrow configuration and obtained essentially the same rates as in our previous experiments. As far as I am aware the design of no full-scale plants was influenced by my incorrect contention but this does not relieve my embarrassment when I think about the matter.

Around 1967 I went on a visit to India arranged by the World Health Organization to discuss collaboration in research in public health engineering projects. Our leader was WHO's Dr Pavanello and the party included the late Dr Sam Jenkins (formerly of the Birmingham, Tame and Rea Drainage Board), Professor Hillel Shuval (an Israeli virology expert) and Mr C D (Guy) Parker (from Australia). Plate 15 shows the party. The visit afforded an opportunity to see some of the main tourist attractions in Delhi including the handsome Lutyens designed Government Offices, the Presidential Building and the Red Fort; and also to go to Agra to see the Taj Mahal and the nearby Fort there. I went by car to Agra with Professor Shuval and Dr Pavanello's secretary. The journey was slightly alarming because our driver, a Sikh, appeared at times to take little account of the safety of the many peasant pedestrians who were trudging along the roads. My apprehensions were considerably diverted, however, by Professor Shuval's proficiency as a splendid raconteur. One of his jokes remains in my mind to this day. It concerns two foreign gentlemen visiting the UK for the first time and on the way practising their English on one another. One said, 'You know my wife is a baroness.' The other replied, 'No, you must have got that wrong: a baroness is an English titled lady.' The first one said, 'Ah yes, what I meant to say was that my wife cannot have children.' The other one said, 'Then what you should have said is that your wife is unbearable.' The first one then said, 'No, this time you've got it wrong. What I should have said is that my wife is inconceivable.' Finally the second one said, 'No I'm sure that's not right. What you should have said is that your wife is impregnable!'

On the last evening of the visit we went out to dinner at a Tandoori restaurant and during the night I was afflicted by 'Delhi belly'. I felt so ill that at one stage on the following morning I thought I should not be able to travel. However Guy Parker gave me one of the pills that he

12. The WHO party visiting Delhi in 1967.

was carrying to combat this type of event and this worked well enough
for me to take the return flight home.

Another of my commitments around this time was to attend
meetings of an Organization for European Cooperation and
Development (OECD) Committee, concerned with pollution control
at a handsome chateau in Paris. I recall the Committee, which mainly
consisted of senior and often elderly European scientists, being joined
by two young and rather ebullient Americans. Their contributions
often seemed to irk the French scientists who appeared only too ready
to put forward counter-arguments. The only other thing that sticks in
my mind is that one of the visits gave me the opportunity to visit the
Folies Bergères. It was a good show though no better I thought than
those I had gone to in Blackpool in my schooldays, even though the
ladies were only half-dressed!

Also in 1967, the late Arthur Key (CBE), Chief Scientist in the
Ministry of Housing and Local Government, jointly with me prepared

a paper on 'Development of Techniques and Administration of Water Pollution Control in the United Kingdom' for the so-called 'Water for Peace' Conference in Washington. It was a pleasure to collaborate with Arthur in this event because quite rightly he was regarded as something of an icon in UK water circles – indeed I recall the late Sir Hugh Fish (former Chief Executive of the Thames Water Authority) referring to him as 'the wisest man in the country in the administration of water technology'. As it transpired some other commitment prevented Arthur from accompanying me to Washington but the paper was well received, which pleased him when I reported this to him on my return. Sadly I cannot now recall anything else about the conference and its aftermath.

To a degree this is in contrast with my next visit to Washington, which was as a member of a small team mustered by Sir Solly Zuckermann (now Lord Zuckermann) who was then the Government's Chief Scientific Adviser (CSA) to exchange ideas with the President's CSA (Lee Dubridge) about water management and pollution control. If memory serves also in the team were Norman (later Sir Norman) Rowntree, Director of the UK's Water Resources Board, and Dr Alan Robinson, Director of the Warren Spring Laboratory (a sister station of WPRL, in the Ministry of Technology and later DoE, also based in Stevenage). I'll have to confess to being slightly disappointed when I realized that the meetings were to take place not in the White House itself but in the White House Offices, a building 'round the back'. Whether anything specific ever evolved from our discussions I do not know but the whole event was a fascinating experience.

I had given a paper about research to the Institution of Municipal Engineers in 1965 and then two years later with the late Dr J D (Doug) Swanwick as my co-author I presented another on treatment and disposal of sewage sludge, a topic on which Doug Swanwick was a notable expert. The second paper was presented to a conference of the Institution in Leeds and resulted in Doug and I being awarded the

Institution's Bronze Medal. Mentioning Doug reminds me that a few years after I went into private practice he did the same and our paths crossed in Indonesia, where he did some substantial work. I'm sure all who knew him will have been much saddened by his death at a relatively early age.

In 1968 I presented the opening paper in a Conference in Milan entitled 'Acqua per il domani (Water for Tomorrow) reviewing Pollution Control and Related Research in UK'. I wrote the paper in English but on this occasion the organizers (Federazione delle Associazioni Scientifiche e Techniche) accompanied its publication with a translation into Italian. Any readers who have stayed the course this far will not be surprised to learn that yet again I cannot remember anything of significance about the conference itself. What I do recall is strolling past a series of booths erected for some sort of international trade fair taking place simultaneously. At one of them a chef was preparing pancakes on a large hotplate in order to make Crêpes Suzette. On the bench supporting the hotplate stood a bottle with a white earthenware stopper looking just like the bottles of vinegar available at the fish-and-chip shop in St Annes that I used to frequent in my youth. The Italian bottle, of course, contained the Grand Marnier, which one applied in whatever dosage one wanted by inverting the bottle and shaking it, just as we did with the vinegar at the chip shop. Perhaps the outcome of this explains why I cannot remember anything of the conference.

Also in 1968 I was scheduled to take part in an international pollution control conference in Prague, but because of the Russian invasion the conference was postponed. It eventually took place the following year and my role was to act as co-chairman in one session of the proceedings. My co-chairman turned out to be a Russian, whose name was something like Lozanski. He spoke very good English, which he told me he had learned in part by listening to the BBC's overseas service. He went on to say, 'I have to acknowledge that we Russians are not very popular over here so you'd better do all the talking.' As it turned out I did. The conference was quite successful, and afforded me the opportunity to stroll through some of the better known parts of the city (Wenceslas Square, the Cathedral, the Palace and the Charles Bridge) whose great attractiveness was at that time however being prejudiced by significant atmospheric corrosion on some of the buildings. I also bought an attractive statuette from a local store, as a memento, and it still stands on the table in the hallway of our house.

In 1969 I acted as consulting editor for a book entitled *Water Pollution Control Engineering* prepared by the Central Office of Information for the Board of Trade. It was originally prepared for distribution in the USA and Canada at the time of the Water Pollution Control Federation's annual conference in Dallas, Texas. Several of its chapters were contributed by members of the Laboratory, including one by myself on Research Services.

Also around that time I was appointed as chairman of a working group set up by the Natural Environment Research Council to advise on the needs for research on problems associated with the eutrophication (nutrient enrichment and its consequences) of natural waters. In the final meeting of the working group I remember becoming overly embarrassed by a question from the floor that I couldn't seem to answer satisfactorily and I felt that I had conducted that part of the meeting poorly. However I was reasonably satisfied with the Report that we produced and a subsequent paper I published in a journal ('Water Treatment and Examination') giving an account of our activities. Looking recently at the published account of the discussion paper I think I would be justified in concluding that broadly our main conclusions were upheld.

In another incident around this time a phone call to my office in the morning informed me that a cargo ship, the *Germania*, carrying chemicals, had foundered in the Channel and drums of the chemicals were being washed up on Cornish beaches. I was therefore to get myself as quickly as possible to Heathrow to fly to the area with Mr

Eldon (now Sir Eldon) Griffiths, Under-Secretary of State at the
Department of the Environment, and one or two other technical
advisers and support staff. We flew in an executive jet (very posh) to a
military airfield in Cornwall arriving just after dark. The following
morning I was detailed to accompany a team of naval demolition
experts who were blowing up those drums that were thought to
contain chemicals of relatively low toxicity. Most of these contained
combustible and I believe largely innocuous organics such as solvents
and feedstock reagents from which more complex chemicals would be
synthesized. They blew up with a bright flash and satisfying bang.
Potentially more dangerous suspect containers had been taken off to a
Government facility, with experience in dealing with toxic chemicals.
My role was simply to assess as best I could the possible pollution
hazards and advise the Minister thereon prior to him addressing local
authorities and the general public on the extent of the problem and
the actions being taken to prevent significant adverse effects. I
considered that pollution hazards were small and that what was being
done would achieve the stated objective. This proved to be the case
and within a day or two the incident had disappeared from the
headlines.

Another event that I recall from this period was attending one of the
Royal Garden Parties at Buckingham Palace. This was an enjoyable
occasion, though the Gardens were crowded with other invitees and
we had no more than a glimpse of the Royal Party.

One notable event in 1969 was the visit to the Laboratory of the
MHLG and Welsh Office Working Party on Sewage Disposal, 'the
Jeger Committee' as we used to call it because its 'Chairman' was the
MP Mrs Lena Jeger. Many members of the Working Party were old
friends or professional acquaintances and its Technical Secretary was
my good friend and former colleague, Geoff Truesdale, who by then
had moved into the Ministry of Housing and Local Government. In
my humble opinion the committee did a good job culminating in
their Report (published in 1970) entitled 'Taken for Granted'

focussing on the need to transform 'a Cinderella of the public services', as Lena Jeger described it in her foreword, into a feature requiring urgent concern.

In 1970 I was one of four co-authors of a paper prepared mainly by the late V K Collinge, David Newsome (both of the Water Resources Board) and J Renold of the Local Government Operational Research Unit (LGORU) describing 'An Economic Model for a Polluted River System'. The aim of the model was to indicate the best way of using the water resources of the River Trent to meet expected future demands in the Midlands and more easterly regions. A major objective of pollution control in the UK had been, and indeed still is, to prevent the release of effluents or changes in hydraulic regime rendering the water unsuitable for the uses to which the community wished it to be put. It was recognized that composition could be varied over a range without affecting suitability for use but the ranges for given uses had not hitherto been defined in a holistic manner. The excellent contribution that David Newsome and his LGORU co-workers made was to specify the concentration ranges defining the 'quality states' permitting given uses in this way; and then to model the impact of possible changes in polluting loads or hydraulic regimes on these quality states, throughout the river systems. Once having predicted quality states the cost and benefits associated with achievement of any given quality state could then be estimated. Though the model was in a sense ground-breaking, decisions on whether or not (and in this case not) to use the Trent as a source for potable supply in the event turned on uncertainty as to the possible release of potentially hazardous but not easily detected substances to the river from industry. Nevertheless the model provided a guideline as to what might effectively be done in less complex situations or those in which much more detail on industrial discharges was available.

We had numerous distinguished visitors to the Laboratory. The first of those that I remember was Lord Hailsham though this was before the period of my Directorship. He listened quietly and with evident interest to what I had to tell him about the work my section and I were engaged in and quite belied his political mace-wielding flamboyance. Then there was the MP Mrs Lena Jeger, Peter Shore (who took lunch with us in the Lab canteen) and Anthony Wedgwood Benn (in his capacity as Minister of Technology). When he arrived Mr Benn first went briefly into the downstairs toilets and then when beginning his address to us in the conference room on the third floor amused us by saying that he was sorry for the delay but he had had to make his contribution to the pollution problem.

The most interesting visit to the Laboratory occurred in 1970 when the then Prime Minister, the Rt Hon Mr Harold Wilson (later Sir Harold and then Baron Wilson of Rievaulx) visited the Laboratory accompanied by the Secretary of State for Local Government and Regional Planning, Mr Anthony Crosland, and Sir Solly (later Lord) Zuckermann. They toured the Lab during the morning taking a keen interest in what we had to tell and show them. Lunch was then taken at our sister station's (The Warren Spring Laboratory's) (WSL) staff dining room, virtually just across the road. I was invited to join the luncheon party to accompany the WSL Director, Dr Alan Robinson. Over lunch the PM and Mr Crosland made pleasant conversation with us. To me the PM came across as much more a patriotic Yorkshireman than a Labour politician, though of course to what extent this reflected the politician's art or a true impression I shall never know. I think it was just after lunch when we were joined briefly by Mrs Shirley Williams (the then MP for Stevenage) and now Baroness Williams. Mrs Williams came across to WPRL with me when I returned, in order to discuss with me a pollution problem that had been raised by one of her constituents. Plate 13 shows the party leaving WSL. Alan Robinson is on the extreme right with to the left of him behind the PM John Alabaster (of our staff), Anthony Crosland and Sir Solly.

Later in 1970 I attended the IAWPR Biennial Conference in San Francisco. In opening the conference the keynote speech, a very good

13. Saying goodbye to the Prime Minister, Mr Harold Wilson, at the
Warren Spring Laboratory, 1970.

one delivered in impeccable style, was given by Mrs Shirley Temple
Black, the former world-renowned actress who at the time was the
US 'ambassador' to the UN Environmental Programme. It was a
typically good conference scientifically and my participation afforded
opportunities to see some of the very interesting wastewater treatment
facilities in the region. From a less technical standpoint I was pleased
to be able to shake hands with Ronald Reagan, who visited the
conference (with his minders) in his capacity then of Governor of
California. But that was as nothing compared with the pleasure that I
and one or two other Brits had in having about five minutes' chat with
Shirley Temple later in the day. She looked very charming and came
across to us as something of an Anglophile telling us that she often
spent time in London.

I can't now be sure whether it was on the initial stages of this visit
or another occasion when I stopped off in San Francisco before taking

a helicopter flight to Berkeley (University of California) to see one of
the leading figures in coastal pollution research at the time, the late
Professor E A (Tiny) Pearson, so-called Tiny because of his huge size
(in 3 dimensions). I remember, because it was the first time I had
flown in a 'chopper', being quite surprised when the rear of the craft
rose before the nose; and subsequently being enthralled by the view as
we flew over San Francisco Bay. Other memories of San Francisco
include the usual tourist's visit to Fisherman's Wharf, having lunch in
the restaurant at the top of 'the Mark', and again being surprised when
either on that tower or the 'skyscraper' next door the lift was on the
outside of the building.

I think it was just before the conference that I went with Mr D H
Price, then in the Ministry of Housing and Local Government, who
was an old friend with whom I had served on several Government
Committees spanning quite a number of years, to visit the sewage
treatment plant at South Lake Tahoe (Plate 18). We stayed in Tahoe
City, which has the curious feature that, so I understood, it is crossed
by the Nevada state boundary line, on one side of which Las Vegas
style gambling is permitted and on the other it is not. David and I took
dinner in a restaurant near the Casino watching, as we passed by,
numerous gamblers operating one-armed bandits. When we came
down for breakfast the following morning we were convinced that
some of the same people we had seen the night before were once
more still trying their luck.

On a more serious note we were quite impressed with the Tahoe
plant, which was very much 'state-of-the-art' at the time. It had been
designed to treat the wastewaters to a very high standard in order to
prevent any impact on the highly picturesque Lake, the waters in
which are amongst the three most clear in the world (Plate 19). It was
said that if one dropped a dinner plate into the water it could be seen
on the bottom at least 30 ft below. However despite the fact that the
plant effluent would probably have met the target objective the local
authorities prudently conveyed it to a small impounding reservoir

which, if memory serves, was then used as a source for local industries.

1970 was also the year in which I made my first of many visits to Australia. This came about largely I think by prompting at the Department by the late Douglas Thistlethwayte of the Australian Water and Wastewater Association during a trip to UK. Doug's wife Molly is, like Kath, a keen amateur painter and we keep in touch regularly at Christmas time.

I remember arriving in Sydney airport not long after Tony Jacklin had flown in but without his clubs, which had somehow gone astray. I was pretty travel weary but was immediately confronted by a young lady television interviewer wearing dark glasses, who thrust a microphone at me and said something along the lines of, 'Prince Charles said that Bondi Beach was not in good condition. What do you think?' Fortunately, as I had not then been to Bondi I was able to dodge what otherwise might have been a controversial subject. I gave two more TV interviews during the visit which included time with the British High Commissioner, trips to research units in Melbourne and Sydney, and a brief tour in Tasmania.

In Canberra I gave a public lecture about current pollution control and related research at the 'space-ship like' Academy of Science (Plate 19). In Melbourne I gave a 15-minute radio broadcast. I wrote what I had planned to say and showed it to the programme director. His response was to say, 'Well it's no doubt good sound stuff, but it's rather boring isn't it; can't you introduce a few rhetorical questions?' Rather chastened I endeavoured to do just that. Talking about it afterwards with a senior member of the Melbourne Metropolitan Board of Works he indicated that he thought it had come across quite well, but rather like me he was an 'establishment man', not much into histrionics.

In the spring of 1972 we held, at the Laboratory, a symposium on 'Mathematical and Hydraulic Modelling of Estuarine Pollution' at which 19 papers were presented. I chaired the opening session and wrote a Foreword to the Proceedings which were published by DoE later in the year. My former boss Bill Southgate chaired the final session and as it happened Ted Flaxman whom I joined as a Partner in B & P just under 2 years later was a participant. The symposium showed that techniques of modelling estuaries had developed considerably but the number of successful applications was still quite few.

After the introduction of the defence research establishment into the Ministry of Technology, we (Directors) met at intervals to discuss matters of common interest. These meetings brought me into contact with a good many people that I would otherwise probably have never met. One of those I particularly remember was Sir Robert Cockburn, the Director at Farnborough. On one occasion he invited other Directors and their wives to the Farnborough Air Show. He had a hospitality tent just alongside the end of the main runway and from near the tent we watched in awe, and some trepidation, while jets travelling at not much below the speed of sound belted down towards us in a truly exhilarating display. I also met one of Sir Robert's colleagues (whose name now regrettably escapes me) who had been working on the design of Concorde. At my request he came to give a talk at the Lab. He began this by saying, 'Drip, drip, drip…bang!' emphasizing the 'bang' by slapping down a notebook and then explaining that the consequences of a small leak in a supersonic aircraft could be catastrophic. I found this so arresting that I recounted the experience in opening my Presidential Address to the Institute of Water Pollution some years later.

On another occasion I went to the Water Resources Board's offices to a meeting organized by Norman Rowntree to advise His Royal Highness The Duke of Edinburgh on recent developments in water management. The Duke had his arm in a sling, as a result I believe of a mishap playing polo. My role was to tell the Duke in a short 10-minute presentation about the recovery of water suitable for potable use from sewage effluent.

The Duke was clearly interested in improvement in pollution control. In this context I recall a brief conversation with him some years later, when he attended a CIWEM dinner, in his capacity as Royal Fellow. He remarked that however good present practice was it didn't contrive to maintain the composition of the water downstream of discharges of treated effluent exactly the same as it would have been in their absence. However, though this is undeniable it is quite feasible, leaving aside benefit-cost considerations, to maintain the suitability of the water downstream of effluent discharges for given uses in the same condition (quality-state) as in the water upstream; and as time goes on this is being achieved with increasing frequency.

Then at the IWPC Annual Conference towards the end of 1973 (and as it turned out towards the end of my time in DoE research) I gave a paper in collaboration with David Price who had by then become DoE's Assistant Director to the Director-General of Water Engineering and had also been awarded a CBE. The paper reviewed the likely developments in relevant environmental R & D programmes likely to take place under the auspices of the then recently enlarged EEC. We concluded that, given various provisos, the UK seemed well placed to contribute substantially to community needs by provision of research and information services; and to benefit from knowledge gained in collaborative work and in respect of increased demand for consultancy services and equipment.

During 1972 the Department of the Environment and the Welsh Office had announced that a new Water Research Centre (WRc) would be established in the spring of 1974 to coincide with a major reorganization of the water industry into ten Regional Water Authorities (RWAs); and that the WRc would incorporate the Water Research Association, the Laboratory (WPRL) and the R & D units of the Water Resources Board and the Directorate General of Engineering. The status proposed for the WRc was similar to that of a research association, partly financed by the RWAs and partly by its other members.

Towards the end of 1973 these intentions were put in hand and I was invited among others to apply for a post including the top post of Director. Shortly before I was due to be interviewed I received a phone call from DoE's Director General of Research, J (Joe) Lyons (JL) in which he said that the 'clean water' lobby was much stronger than the 'dirty water' one and the former were determined to have their man, the Director of WRA, Dr Ron Allen, as Director of the new WRc; then when he retired they'd probably look outside. Leaving personalities aside there was some logic to this as the WRc would be a research association similar in its functions to WRA; though to my mind this did not outweigh the fact that WPRL was substantially larger than WRA and in my view had a much more impressive track record of success in solving research problems in an appreciably more complex field. JL then went on to ask whether I would be prepared to serve under Dr Allen. His question bothered me because I thought, possibly misguidedly, that if I said, 'No' the Laboratory might be divided with part going to the new WRc and part remaining in DoE, probably becoming an adjunct to the Warren Spring Laboratory. Moreover at that stage I wasn't certain whether I would have any other option. So somewhat lamely I replied in the affirmative. However as it happened a strong possibility of another option soon emerged because in talking about the forthcoming events with Peter Norris, one of the Partners of Binnie & Partners (B & P), one of the oldest and most respected UK consulting firms, specializing exclusively in water projects, I became aware that joining the firm was a future possibility.

With these thoughts and my conversation with JL in my mind I took my interview in somewhat 'gung-ho' fashion feeling that I was beaten before I started. I recall saying no doubt quite unwisely (in a political sense) that I would look into the possibility of transferring WRA and the other much smaller units of WRB to WPRL, which was the only site that had the status of a major national laboratory. In my mind there were justifications for this possibility though I see nothing

14. Kath and I receiving a farewell gift from the Staff at WPRL.

to be gained now by detailing them here. Unsurprisingly when the panel announced their decision they confirmed that Dr Allen would be the new Director and they could offer me my then present post. 'Charming condescension' I thought.

However, within a few weeks I had meetings with B & P Partners, said that I would be much interested in joining them as a Partner and to my great pleasure they invited me to do just that – and of course I accepted.

Just before leaving the Laboratory for the last time the staff very kindly presented Kath and me with a very nice Spode plate as shown in Plate 14.

In some ways I felt a bit of a heel for leaving just prior to the major reorganization the effects of which on their future working lives was unpredictable at least in the longer term. However several factors had influenced my decision to go. One was that I was confident that my Assistant Director, George Eden, would manage the Laboratory very well. Another was the impact of my conversation with JL. Unfortunately I didn't feel able to disclose this to the staff who, if they had felt let down by me would presumably have felt less so had they known. Additionally I had been conscious that my time was increasingly being taken up with committees, 'pushing paper around', and other administrative matters, whereas I had a hankering for a more active role 'at the sharp end', which I saw as being forthcoming if I took up consultancy; and affording me greater opportunity to turn from research to application of research results.

As things transpired the opposite of my hopes of centring WRc on the Stevenage site occurred in that the Laboratory was eventually sold off by WRc and the building demolished to make way for an ice rink; a travesty in my view bearing in mind its past position in the seventies as arguably the best pollution control research laboratory in the world. As a further irony I understand that the Centre is now virtually totally concentrated on one site, that of the Engineering facility that had been built at Swindon shortly after the formation of WRc. This was an additional irony for me because on the few occasions when at WPRL we had identified engineering issues that we thought would merit research we were instructed by Headquarters to 'back-off', as this was the province of the Construction Industries Research Association (CIRIA).

CHAPTER 6

Private Practice as a Partner: 1974-86

I COUNTED MYSELF very fortunate to have been admitted to Partnership in the excellent practice of Binnie & Partners. The firm had an enviable reputation stemming from design and supervision of construction of a huge range of water based infrastructure in the UK and overseas including dams, reservoirs, hydroelectric schemes, water and wastewater treatment facilities, drainage and water supply networks; and from related master plans and similar strategic studies. A history of the Partnership, founded by Sir Alexander Binnie in 1890, is given in a publication by Mr A C (Alan) Twort, who was a colleague throughout the whole of my time in the firm. All fourteen of the existing Partners were skilled professionals with excellent track records and their individual achievements were well on a par with those of the many senior people I had met in my previous service in Government research.

Perhaps inevitably against this background I initially felt myself as being something of an 'also ran'. This was essentially because the success of the firm depended on the revenue derived from our services and whereas that from projects involving construction of major engineering facilities was commensurately large that from the sort of science-based projects that I thought I might be able to secure could by comparison be described as 'peanuts'. However I beavered away to the best of my ability in endeavouring to complement the work of the other Partners and increase the diversity of the firm's activities; and fortunately before long I was able to gain one or two worthwhile projects.

One notable difference from my previous career was that I soon found myself involved in more entertaining and especially in a great deal more travelling. Fortunately as it happened partners and the most senior staff of the firm travelled First Class when I joined in 1974 and that remained the case until around 1982. By that time the market for services in the UK had declined considerably, partly as a result of privatization and because we then had to do much more travelling, prospecting for and carrying out work overseas, our travel costs had risen to such an extent that we switched to Business Class when flying. This didn't bother me in the least because with my dimensions I was just as comfortable in a Business Class as in a First Class seat; of course deep-vein thrombosis had hardly been heard of in those days.

During my time with the firm I worked in some 35 countries though mostly for quite short periods. Indeed I think my longest unbroken stay was for nine weeks in Australia. To avoid the difficulty and fragmentation of putting all these visits plus activities in UK into a historical sequence I have divided what follows for the most part into events in UK and Eire and independently those in each individual overseas country. In so doing I have not adopted any rigorous sequence, such as alphabetical order, but have presented them in a rough succession from those in which I spent the most time to those in which my involvements were very short or in one case did not involve visiting the country at all.

UK and Eire

On becoming a Partner one of my first responsibilities was to oversee the work of the firm's chemical and biological laboratory and its team of an engineer and several scientists who hitherto had mainly worked in the field of water treatment. This team was led by our Associate Mr F W (Frank) Crowley OBE. Frank had been involved in the design of treatment plants in various parts of the world, especially Malaysia where he had worked for several years before joining the firm. His name appears on the plaque outside the Admin buildings of plants I have visited in Malaysia, acknowledging his part in their design. He was deservedly appointed a Partner in the firm following my retirement from the Partnership. Other members of the team included the late F E (Frank) Wallingford, Brian Hoyle, Claire Jackson, all chemists, Don Ratnayaka, a chemical engineer, Keith Herber, an engineer, and Alvin Smith, a biologist. This team had been involved in the design of numerous water treatment plants in the UK and overseas and there was little need for me to become engaged technically in that part of the firm's work.

One other consequence of my 'change of life' was that I became the representative of Consultant Members of the WRc on the Centre's Council, endeavouring to make sure that our interests were taken into account in framing the research programme.

My work in the UK was punctuated by many overseas visits and otherwise consisted mainly of short and diverse inputs into a wide variety of projects but often involving the personnel in the WT Department. One of my first assignments actually took place almost entirely overseas but since it was arranged in the UK and consisted essentially of a tour with short stays in various countries I deal with it here for convenience.

This was a project for a UN working Group, that took me to Pakistan, India, Iran (Teheran) and the Philippines (Manila) and finally Canada (Ottawa). I went with an American Professor, C P ('Connie') Straub, to examine the scope for further research into ways of providing water supplies and sanitation for rural communities. By coincidence Professor Straub had worked in the radiochemical field in the USA at about the time that I was doing similar work in the UK.

At the start of our tour when in Pakistan we were staying in a hotel in Lahore and I was invited to lunch at the Club of a local academic whom I had met professionally in the UK and I think also in Delft. Fruit and salad were on the menu and I remember thinking at the time that I hoped they had been washed in chlorinated water. As a precaution I took a tablet that I had been prescribed in London as an 'antidote', the name of which now escapes me. Despite this the following day I awoke feeling very uncomfortable and at breakfast to my embarrassment I was violently sick over the hotel floor. I went straightaway to a local doctor who asked me what I had been prescribed. When I told him he said, 'Oh no, Sahib, not nearly strong enough!' He then prescribed what I think was tetracycline. Whatever it was it seemed to do the trick and I was able to continue without further incident.

In India I encountered for the first time an experience that was apparently quite common among developed country personnel when photographing village communities. This was that the children shied away when a camera was pointed at them, never having seen such a device before. Those in the picture (Plate 21) were clearly more experienced. Also in India I had the pleasure of visiting the Central Public Health Environmental Research Institute in Nagpur and a unit of the same organisation in Calcutta. On the technical side our subsequent experiences in Iran were similar to those in Pakistan and India. Manila was a little different in that we visited a local unit working actively on the problems of 'technology transfer'.

Finally we delivered our findings in Ottawa. Perhaps not surprisingly we did not come up with any revolutionary proposals. We considered that, although there was scope for intensifying research already in progress, what was wanted was not so much a great deal more research but wider application of the best features of available technology. As has often been the case the real problem was shortage of funds rather than lack of technical knowledge. The idea that in some fields more research will produce nigh-on miraculous solutions can often be misplaced.

I enjoyed my short stay in Canada. One or two things quite surprised me. The first was that, having had to break my journey to Ottawa in Montreal, I found it easier to order my lunch in an airport café by speaking my pidgin French than by using English. Also in Ottawa, after having admired the green roofs of the Government buildings I was taken on my first visit to what I was told was a genuine

15. One of Kath's paintings of Amsterdam.

*16. The Laboratory's powered catamaran used for studying dispersion
in coastal waters.*

17. Measuring aspects of Water Quality in the Severn Estuary by Helicopter.

18. The wastewater treatment plant near Lake Tahoe, California.

19. Lake Tahoe, California.

20. The Academy of Science, Canberra.

79

21. Children at a village well in India c. 1974.

22. The desalination plant at Lok on Pai, Hong Kong.

23. At the edge of one of the reed-beds at Windelsbleiche, Germany.

24. Receiving the IAWPRC's Karl Imhoff and Pierre Koch medal from the late Professor Poul Harremoës.

26. Mining facilities at Cerro de Pasco, Peru 1974.

25. Mining facilities at Cerro de Pasco, Peru 1974.

27. Flying over New South Wales c. 1975.

28. Open-cast uranium mining area in central USA.

29. Trial open-cast uranium mining area, Yeelirrie, Western Australia.

30. Maunsell's Bridge on the River Tamar, Tasmania.

31. Suzhou Creek at the confluence with the River Huangpu, Shanghai.

32. Part of the River Huangpu, Shanghai.

33. Kath, Gill and I at a dinner c. 1975.

34. My mother, Mrs Dorothy Downing, with our two Labradors, c. 1980.

35. On the river near Chongqing, China.

*36. With Graham Thompson and David Macdonald in the
Forbidden City, China.*

*37. A Chinese team monitoring water quality in the
Mi Yun reservoir near Beijing.*

38. Alan George and I with a Chinese lady counterpart in Beijing.

39. Part of Tolo Harbour, Hong Kong.

*40. Kath with Tony Pitman and his wife at Skukuza in the
Kruger National Park, 1980.*

41. Looking over Sha Tin towards Tolo Harbour, Hong Kong.

42. Near Hermanus Golf Club, South Africa.

43. With Professor Takeshi Kubo in the B & P office in Redhill.

44. Impact of wastewater discharges on coastal waters near Napier-Hastings, New Zealand c. 1974.

45. Napier-Hastings chief engineer during our tour of the North Island of New Zealand.

46. The Kali Sunter near its exit to the sea in Jakarta, Indonesia.

Japanese restaurant. I remember sitting round a huge hotplate on which our meat was cooked. I didn't encounter anything like that in my brief subsequent visits to Japan.

Then for the same reasons as for the 'Rural Communities' project I mention here that towards the end of 1974 I went to the offices of the Food and Agriculture Organisation (FAO) in Rome for a preliminary meeting of a Working Group of GESAMP (Group of Experts on the Scientific Aspects of Marine Pollution) charged with defining 'Principles for Developing Coastal Water Quality Criteria'. Then in 1975, as a member of the Group, I went to Dubrovnik for a few days to help finish our assignment. Our meetings were chaired by Dr J S (John) Alabaster who, as I have mentioned earlier, was one of my former colleagues at WPRL. My role, quite a minor one, included preparation of a paper entitled 'Criteria for Protection of Amenities' bearing on the impact of pollution on the visual aesthetic satisfaction afforded by coastal water. This contributed in a small way to a final report published by FAO in Rome the following year.

The visit to Dubrovnik afforded an opportunity to see something of the magnificent walled city, which I believe is the oldest of its kind in the world (and I hope has not suffered significant damage in the recent war). The splendid scenery and wealth of impressive architecture are very well displayed in a book about the city that I was given as a memento during our visit.

Also in 1975 with the aid I think of recommendations made by Geoff Truesdale and the late Fred Lester (OBE) (of the Severn-Trent Water Authority) I felt very honoured to be awarded the Dunbar Gold Medal (Dunbar being an early pioneer in wastewater treatment) by a body that organized water industry exhibitions and associated conferences but later evolved into the European Water Association. I gathered that the prize was actually 10,000 Deutschmarks of which 3000 were devoted to the medal. I remember asking Fred and Geoff shortly before going to Munich to collect the award whether (apart obviously from my thanks) there was anything special I ought to say at the ceremony. 'Yes,' said Fred, with typical humour, 'Wo sind die Deutschmärke?' By coincidence in opening up the Diploma accompanying the award recently, for the first time in nearly 30 years, I came across several other items that I had totally forgotten, and though out of historical context, they fit in here as well as anywhere. One was a Certificate of Achievement issued to me in 1966 by the Institute of Advanced Sanitation Research International, an American organization. Another was a document dated March 1964 given to me by the American Association of Professors in Sanitary Engineering certifying that I had completed a Visiting Lecturer Tour of American Universities. One of the signatures on the document was that of Professor Richard Dick who either before or afterwards spent a sabbatical year with us at WPRL. Kath and I still keep in touch at Christmas with Richard and his wife Dolores. Another US 'sabbatical visitor' was Professor John Andrews with his wife, Marge, with whom we also keep in touch. A third document was a Diploma certifying that in 1972 I had been elected a Fellow of the Faculty of Building. Additionally there were two letters (which in this case I hadn't forgotten), one from the *Sunday Times* and the other from the *Sunday Telegraph* informing me that I had won the respective weekend cryptic crossword competitions. For the last 20 years or so I have been a regular *Times* crossword addict, indeed it seems to have got to the point where I can't start my breakfast until I've done at least a few clues. However I still haven't won in the weekend 'standard' puzzle or the associated Jumbo but I continue to live in hopes.

Another early involvement was assisting one of my Partners, Ted Flaxman, in the design of extensions to the Anglian Water Authority's Peterborough Sewage Treatment works. As it was one of my first assignments after moving into private practice I hoped that it might be possible to produce a design that would offer some advantage over traditional practice. Thus my initial proposal was to provide secondary treatment in a uniformly-mixed 'activated sludge' plant, the argument for which I saw as being the opportunity to minimize energy consumption by relatively straightforward automatic control of dissolved-oxygen levels in the reactors. What prompted this suggestion was mainly the results of the experiments we had performed at WPRL on settlement of the biomass (the activated sludge) that I mentioned earlier. I considered that providing we maintained low loadings the settleability of the sludge would be satisfactory. However the head of our client's technical team, Bill Smith (with whom Ted and I were on good terms not least because of being fellow members of IWPC) was convinced that a more conventional baffled configuration would be much more reliable and of course as the client's representative his view prevailed. As time has gone on the practice of designers has certainly more and more been to opt for baffled configurations, especially because the technology of automatic control of aeration has advanced considerably (not least as a consequence of work my colleagues, especially Mr R (Ron) Briggs, had done at WPRL) and incidence of poor settleability could justifiably be regarded as the Achilles heel of the process. I must admit this was probably right, though I can't help wishing that someone had repeated the experiments we did at low loadings in larger plants and with diurnally varying flows.

Mentioning Ron Briggs reminds me that Ron and his charming wife Betty were very good ballroom dancers, who in my early times at Stevenage ran a dancing class that Kath and I attended. This brought us up to a standard at which we could at least take to the floor without feeling overtly embarrassed. As it happened, now nearly 40 years ago, Ron and Betty bought the house that we then lived in in Knebworth and like us are still inhabiting our then new properties. If memory serves I think Ron subsequently obtained a DSc and went on to become a Professor at the City University, London.

Another interesting though short assignment was in advising ICI Ltd on aspects of the development of a new method of wastewater treatment known as the Deep-Shaft Process. This was in effect a modification of the traditional AS process, so called because it involved injecting the air necessary for biological oxygen into the mixture of wastewater and suspended biomass as it flowed downwards through a U-tube shaped reactor and then back up to the surface. It was possible to get very high rates of oxygen transfer in this way though the advantage of any increase above normal rates would have depended on the micro-organisms utilizing the DO faster, a circumstance that did not occur to any marked extent. Another difference from conventional practice was that in the case of sewage treatment the normal stage of preliminary sedimentation was omitted. At the time ICI were of the opinion that the surplus biomass (sludge) production per unit of BOD removed in the process was significantly below that from conventional plants. However as I pointed out in comparing production from crude sewage with that from settled sewage they were not comparing like with like. Nevertheless the process had interesting potential especially for treating stronger wastes generating high oxygen demands and was adopted for treatment at several sewage and industrial water treatment plants mostly in Japan and one sewage treatment plant in the UK, at Dartford. However it has never caught on widely probably for a complex balance of reasons, of which the disadvantageous ones included the fact that the destruction of organic matter by bio-oxidation much reduced the potential for generation of methane by anaerobic digestion of the sludge, higher rates of air supply, doubts about the settleability of the biomass recycled through the reactor, reaction rates being not much different from those in conventional plants, and costs of construction and maintenance of deep-shafts.

Also around this time I was author of a paper on 'Water quality studies for the Wash Water Storage Scheme' presented to a joint Institution of Civil Engineers and Central Water Planning Unit Symposium at the end of 1976.

On a series of occasions in planning enquiries and legal disputes I acted as an 'Expert Witness' and I deal with a group of them together here though not in historical sequence. Thus the first two of these planning enquiries concerned proposals to build communal industrial waste treatment plants, on countryside sites, one in Hertfordshire and the other in Cambridgeshire near Bury St Edmunds. In both these cases I felt my role to be straightforward in that I considered the facilities proposed were adequate to handle the wastes that were to be treated. My only concern stemmed from the fact that in the latter case the local MP Mr (now Sir) Eldon Griffiths had been as I have mentioned earlier Under Secretary of State at the Department of the Environment, the Department administratively responsible of course for WPRL at the time that I worked there. Although the Department had advocated introduction of such facilities I feared that Sir Eldon might not take kindly to having such a plant 'in his own back yard' so to speak. I need not have worried because in my humble opinion Sir Eldon took a very statesmanlike view of the matter and in the event the proposal in common with that for the Hertfordshire site was given 'the green light'.

I had a similarly satisfactory outcome, though quite different in style, from my participation in a legal action about an odour problem at an industrial waste treatment plant that I had visited a few months before the court case. When I came to give evidence the opposing QC said something along the lines of, 'When you visited the plant Dr Downing you said you didn't find the odour to be offensive'. This nonplussed me because I remembered saying something of the kind and I started to make stumbling attempted explanations and excuses including reference to the fact that I was used to encountering odours of one kind or another in my normal line of business. At this point the Judge said, 'What you mean Dr Downing is, if you say so Mr... (whatever the QC's name was)'. 'Thank you My Lord,' I gasped in relief, 'that's exactly what I should have said.' I found out later that my client's team had been pleased because they felt it indicated that the Judge was persuaded by the rightness of our case and so it proved when he gave his judgement in our favour. The point essentially was that, although there was undoubtedly an odour, whether or not I thought it was not too offensive was irrelevant.

A more amusing experience occurred at an enquiry in Eire when I gave evidence mainly relating to the likely cost of treating a wastewater from a hardboard manufacturing plant in order to reduce the content of sulphate derived from the use of gypsum. The enquiry took place at a hotel about 30 miles north of Dublin in a room which had a large plate glass window overlooking one of the greens of the hotel's 9-hole golf course. As I was sitting facing the window I couldn't help succumbing, from time to time, to the diversion of watching people chipping up to the green, when of course I should have been concentrating on the enquiry. To some extent this mind-wandering was probably induced by the fact that although I had submitted a written Proof of Evidence I was not called on to speak to it. At the end of the day I expressed my surprise at this to our QC, to which he replied, 'To be sure now I didn't call you because we regarded you as our nuclear deterrent!' If I'd thought he was being serious I would have regarded this as one of the best compliments I'd ever received.

Also in the late seventies the firm was appointed to conduct a major study of the feasibility of generating substantial tidal power by using a barrage erected in the Severn Estuary. Stanley Ford was our Partner-in-Charge and Clive Baker, a chief engineer at the time, supervised much of the detailed engineering work. My role was simply to help co-ordinate studies to assess the effects on both water quality and the ecology of the Estuary. To that end I set up an ad hoc guiding committee, which Fred Lester, then Chief Scientist in the Severn-Trent Water Authority, kindly agreed to chair. We were very fortunate to be able to involve the Hydraulics Research Station (Wallingford) (HRS) and the Institution of Marine Environmental Research (IMER) (Plymouth) in the study, these bodies producing an impressive 1-D water quality model and, under the supervision of Dr P J Radford of IMER, probably the first ecosystem model (GEMBASE) for a major water body. Not surprisingly the level of detail in forecasts from

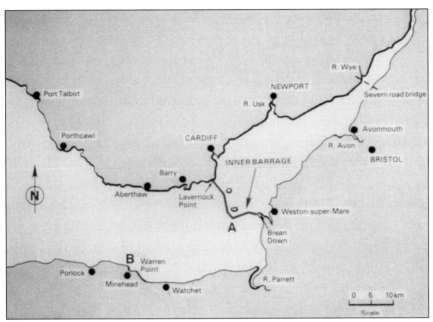

47. The preferred site for a tidal-power barrage on the Severn Estuary.

GEMBASE model was limited to effects on 19 'functional groups' of organisms; there was no possibility at that stage of forecasting effects on individual species. However the model appeared quite adequate for the barrage feasibility study. From an engineering standpoint a study of a range of options led to the conclusion that the preferred scheme would involve construction of a barrage at an 'inner' line from near Weston-super-Mare to Lavernock Point (Plate 47). This was calculated to be capable of generating just over 6% of UK energy requirement at the time. An 'outer' barrage from Minehead to Breaksea Point would have contributed over 9% of the required energy but was proportionally much more expensive. Suffice it to add that in broad terms the water quality and ecosystem models indicated that the introduction of the barrage would not have more than a minor effect on the concentrations of degradable constituents in the Estuary but would probably increase those of conservative pollutants such as cadmium and nickel.

The ecosystem was predicted to be more productive owing to greater penetration of light, following from a reduction in turbidity. At the time introduction of new EC water quality standards was imminent and it seemed evident that to meet them would probably require greater reduction of certain industrial pollutants at source. In particular because the main source of the trace concentration of cadmium in the Estuary appeared to be from atmospheric deposition, probably from the Avonmouth smelters, such releases would have to be at least partially curtailed. Our findings were communicated to a Severn Barrage Committee, whose Chairman was Sir Hermann Bondi (also Chairman of the Natural Environment Research Council at the time). I did not meet with Sir Hermann again until over 20 years later, when at the launch of Sir Martin Holdgate's Memoirs at the Scott Polar Research Centre in Cambridge.

Of course proposals for barrage schemes have long since gone into limbo though whether or not future generations will decide to revive them is a matter for speculation. However, even if all the feasible barrages in the UK were built, they would contribute no more than about 15 per cent of the UK's energy requirement and I am unsure how costs of the energy would compare with that from other sources in today's economic conditions. My personal feeling is that eventually the majority of the requirement may have to be met using nuclear reactors. In that context I cannot help wondering whether there will be scope for accommodating reactors or waste products from them on offshore artificial islands in the style of one engineered by B & P near the Wash – but again that's another story.

In 1978 I was invited by the late Professor Roger Perry to become Visiting Professor in the Public Health Engineering Department of Imperial College, London. I was naturally pleased to be accorded this privilege and did my best to fulfil my expected role over a period of 4 years until 1982. The fact was, however, that I was abroad so much that I was unable to give the assignment as much attention as it needed; and because of inadequate preparation I recall performing rather poorly in the discussion of a lecture I had given in late 1982 to the students and faculty members. Thus when Roger asked me whether I would like to continue for another term I thought it best to resign. As it happened I was succeeded by Ron Packham, a senior member of the Water Research Centre's Medmenham Laboratory (formerly WRA) and someone I had had contacts with over many years. Actually I still meet with Ron at events organised by the Honourable Company of Water Conservators, and we share a common interest in snooker.

Then in 1979 Frank Crowley and I wrote the opening chapter for a DoE and Central Office of Information booklet on Water Treatment Technology the object, of course, being to publicize UK expertise in the provision of water services. Looking at the chapter again recently I am sure that Frank must have written most of it because it largely contains details of facilities in the design of which I played no part, such as the High Island reservoir scheme, the Sha Tin Water Treatment Works, the Lok-on-Pai desalination plant (Plate 22), all in Hong Kong, a treatment plant in New Zealand and the Three Valleys treatment plant and the Farmoor Reservoir in the UK.

In 1979 I became, in succession to Geoff Truesdale, President of the Institution of Water Pollution Control (IWPC) at the Annual Conference in Torquay. At the Conference Dinner held at the Palace Hotel, Mr (now Sir) Eldon Griffiths kindly gave the main speech. The dining room at the time was a good deal wider than it was deep and I can remember Eldon having to look from side to side at his audience when speaking, which caused him to remark that 'it was like being at a tennis match'. Plate 48 shows Kath and me with the Mayor and Mayoress of Torquay before the dinner.

At the conference itself after my Presidential Address, in which I raised several questions about the outlook following privatization, we had a series of papers, including one prepared by Mr D A (Dave) Healey of the Department of Construction in Canberra, David Keiller, and myself reporting the outcome of the project our Australian firm

48. Kath and I with the Mayor and Mayoress of Torquay.

had conducted to assess the needs for nutrient removal in the Lower
Molonglo Treatment Plant (a project I give more detail about in my
account of activities in Australia).

Other principal guests at the conference were by tradition the
President of the American Water Pollution Control Federation and
his lady, in this case Marty Lang and his wife Bertha (Plate 49). They
were quite a lively couple and I recall Bertha at one stage after dinner
playing the piano for us. Additionally, and rather to my surprise,
Marty announced that Geoff Truesdale and myself were henceforth
inducted to form the UK chapter of an American organization known
as the Select Society of Sanitary Sludge Shovellers (the 5Ss).
Essentially this was a society of people who had done well-recognized
useful work in the field of sewage treatment. Members in the USA

49. Kath and I with Marty and Bertha Lang, Torquay 1979.

were expected to wear a small gold-plated shovel-shaped clip on occasions when they were to meet other members; and if when not wearing the shovel they met other shovellers who were, they were supposed to buy them all a drink. In the UK we uphold the shovel-wearing tradition though I have never encountered the drinks penalty. Initially even after I had been appointed Dean, I'll have to confess that I had difficulty in taking the society seriously, and I blush to think that in my year as Dean, due mainly to overseas commitments, I missed a meeting or two. However as time went on the Society expanded, became increasingly meritorious and indeed was instrumental in helping to initiate the formation of a City Livery Company, now the Worshipful Company of Water Conservators. Most of our 5Ss members, now around 50 in number, are either Freemen or Liverymen of the City of London. (Among the privileges of this office is permission to drive a flock of sheep over Tower Bridge!) The Livery Company meanwhile has become increasingly

50. With John and Barbara Calvert c. 1980.

strong and though I don't nowadays get to many of its functions, those I do attend are always enjoyable.

One of our early Deans in the 5Ss was the late Mr J T (John) Calvert, at the time I think Senior Partner of John Taylor's. He is shown in Plate 50 with his wife Barbara. Barbara is the daughter of the late Dr Albert Parker, who before retirement was Director of the former DSIR Fuel Research Station at Greenwich. Barbara is a noted QC, and following remarriage is now Lady Lowry. In John's memory the 5Ss introduced the Calvert Medal, an honour presented to the preceding and succeeding Deans, and thus happily one I hold.

Also in the late seventies after prompting from Richard Warren (whom I mention later) B & P bought the lease of the Arlesey premises of Cross & Bevan, the paper industry consultants to whom I have referred earlier. We re-equipped the existing small laboratory so as to be able to deliver a variety of services in the environmental field including chemical analysis, toxicity testing and laboratory investigations relating to the design of water and effluent treatment plants. The new unit, Binnie Environmental Ltd (BEL), was put under the control of Dr Tony James, the firm's Geotechnical expert, and other members of B & P such as Colin Appleyard and myself were appointed as Directors (non-executive in my case). My role was essentially advisory, though I did get quite closely involved in one or two projects, one I recall requiring design of a facility for nitrifying a waste with a high content of ammonia. The project was carried out by Lynn Smith who later joined our Hong Kong firm. However following the amalgamation of B & P with the US firm Black and Veatch, the new firm sold BEL.

Also during my Presidential Year I took the Chair at a symposium organized by the Institute's Scottish Branch on 'River Pollution Prevention'. The symposium, which took place in Edinburgh, centred on sludge treatment and disposal and brought forth much useful information particularly on incineration and, at the other 'extreme', disposal to sea. George Eden, who at the time was, I think, still Director of the WRc Stevenage laboratory, gave the closing vote of thanks. Additionally in the same year I wrote an article entitled 'Global Needs Drain Declining Resources' for the journal *New Civil Engineer*.

It must have been around this time that I became conscious that George was feeling quite discontented with the progress of events at WRc and had decided to retire. I felt sure that our Partnership could benefit greatly from forming an association with him and accordingly with Partners' approval I invited him to join us as a Consultant. To my great pleasure he accepted the invitation and we worked fruitfully together on a range of projects up until his retirement in the mid nineties.

One of the first examples of this came in another Enquiry when, with George's help, I prepared a Proof of Evidence for Preston Borough Council for a Hearing in the House of Lords, Session 1980-1, regarding the proposed closure of the Port of Preston. Our evidence was concerned with possible effects on the quality of water in the

Ribble Estuary following cessation of the dredging hitherto carried out by the Preston Borough Council. Broadly we concluded that any adverse effects would be minor and given certain eventualities, unquantifiable from the data available, some aspects of water quality would be improved. I believe these conditions were accepted and I was not called to testify in person.

In 1981 I gave the closing address in a conference on 'Coastal Discharges – engineering aspects and experiences' organized by the Institution of Civil Engineers. The Proceedings were published by Thomas Telford Ltd, London. As it happened my Partner, Ted Flaxman, and former colleague, Hugh Gameson, were both on the organizing committee and both gave papers.

In 1982 George Eden and I wrote a paper on 'Water Recycling – Research Needs' that was published in the journal *Water Science and Technology*. This was a wide-ranging overview of some 15 areas we considered appropriate for further research.

By contrast with my previous experience my last involvement in an official Enquiry was a trifle humiliating. The Enquiry concerned an Appeal by a paper mill (my firm's client) against a requirement proposed by the Don River Purification Board (RPB) in Scotland that the firm should treat their effluent sufficiently to meet the so-called 30:20 standard (the numbers referring respectively to the maximum content (in milligrams per litre) of suspended solids and 5-day biochemical oxygen demand). To meet this requirement so-called full secondary biological treatment would be needed. The object was to eliminate from the Don the heavy visible growths of Sphaerotilis (sometimes called 'sewage fungus') that had developed downstream of the effluent outfall. I was reasonably certain that treatment of the wastewaters to the required standard would achieve the desired objective. However I considered that the relationships between effluent quality and Sphaerotilis growth were imperfectly established and that possibly less intensive and thereby less expensive treatment might be adequate. Additionally I felt there were flaws, albeit minor, in the research that the RPB had done to demonstrate that the wastewaters were treatable to the required standard; and that the proposed 'deadline' for introduction of the plant was unrealistically short. I was putting forward my views in response to the opposing QC's questions when he suddenly asked me to perform a calculation. As I started to do so the room went deathly silent and this combined with my being acutely conscious of everyone watching me slowed down my progress. Eventually after what seemed an age I proffered the result of my calculation to the QC, who however made no comment and passed on to some other point. I have good reason to believe from later conversations that the Chairman and his Technical Adviser, both from DoE, considered that the QC's gambit had just been a cynical attempt to stop me in my tracks. I have often wondered subsequently what would have happened if I'd said, 'I'll give my solution to the Chairman if you'll give yours'. However, though my point about the timetable being too short was accepted, the main Appeal was turned down. No doubt this was because what was being asked of the client was no more than a conventional requirement for discharges to rivers and many months of further investigation would have been needed to establish whether or not less rigorous treatment would have sufficed. I remain embarrassed that I did not have the good sense to offer this view strongly enough to our client before the action.

On another occasion I had initially expected to be called to testify in a legal action but in the event I was not. The original circumstances were that when driving home from a conference late at night, I turned on the car radio and just caught the tail end of a report that tragically several people had been killed in an explosion at the opening of a water pumping station. It was not until the following day that I discovered that the pumping station, at Abbeystead in Cumbria, was one that had been designed by my firm albeit shortly before I had joined the practice. It transpired that water supersaturated with methane had migrated upwards from several thousand feet below to the tunnel through which water was conveyed to the pumping station and as a result of the reduction in pressure following the ascent a pocket of methane had been released into the tunnel. When the pumps were switched on the methane was shunted into the pumping station and by ill chance was ignited possibly by someone lighting a cigarette. Probably because I had had only minor involvement in water supply, as distinct from pollution control, I was unaware that something of the kind had happened in the USA a few years previously. A misfortune in the case of Abbeystead was that following what I understood was standard practice, the air in the tunnel during construction was tested for methane but none was detected. In searching for an explanation of the tragedy soon after its occurrence I was led to wonder whether dissolved methane could have been released to the air as water in the pumping station passed over weirs that had been built into its structure. Accordingly with the help of Tony James, I determined the relative rates of transfer of oxygen and methane from water stirred in laboratory vessels, then assuming with good grounds that these relative rates would be independent of the nature of the exposure of the water to the air, I used knowledge of the rate of transfer of oxygen at weirs to estimate the potential rate of release of methane at the weirs in the pumping station. I concluded tentatively that the rate of release of methane from water saturated with the gas at atmospheric pressure might just be enough to produce an explosive mixture in the air in the pumping station. But I was then intending to argue that no one could possibly have foreseen this because the rate of transfer of methane from water to the air at weirs had never previously been explored. However by the time I had done this it had become much clearer that the correct, more obvious, explanation was that the methane had been released from supersaturated solution to form the pocket of gas in the tunnel to which I have already referred. Unsurprisingly therefore I was not called on to offer testimony in the ensuing legal action.

In another assignment, around 1983, I was Partner-in-Charge of a study to recommend the design of extensions to a water treatment plant at Ardleigh, in Essex, drawing its water from an eutrophic reservoir, suffering from excessive algal growths.

In the same year (1983) Frank Crowley and I were awarded the Rex Winter Premium of the then Institution of Water Engineers and Scientists for a paper we had given on 'Some Problems in the Exploitation of Polluted Waters as Sources for Potable Supply'. Among other things this contained accounts of work the WT department in particular had done on supplies from the Bedok Catchment, Singapore, from Lough Neagh, Northern Ireland, from Camiri in Bolivia and from the Swan-Avon Tributaries in Perth, Western Australia.

Then around this time Rodney Squires (to whom I refer later) then in South Africa, introduced a modification to a process that was being researched locally known as cross-flow microfiltration. The essence of this process was that the liquid to be filtered was pumped at high velocity across the surface of the filter so that the shearing action of the flow prevented accumulation of deposited solids to an extent sufficient to interfere significantly with filtration. Rodney's innovation was to replace the perforated solid tube filters hitherto used by flexible fabric. After trials of various potential applications in our laboratory in London we patented the process. We did not see it as having a significant place in conventional water treatment for public supply not least because it would have been far too expensive. Rodney and I gave a paper in 1990 describing experiments that we and others had done to investigate its potential, to an IWEM Symposium at Imperial College on 'Options for Producing Higher Quality Sewage Effluents'. We concluded that although satisfactory filtration had been achieved in initial trials it was too early to assess the future prospects since much would depend on the life of the filter fabric. However there seemed a possibility that the device would have an application for situations where space for conventional filtration was limited as for example in some industrial situations. At the time this work was in progress we also undertook a study to find a solution to a problem that had developed in California in which we saw possible opportunities to use the process. However I deal with this in my subsequent account of work in the USA.

Around 1985 I joined a Long Term Water Research Requirements Committee, chaired by Martin Holdgate, set up as a result of recommendations by the House of Lords Select Committee on Science and Technology. Looking back now over a long list of our recommendations in the final report (April 1986) they all seem sensible and, though I am now badly out of touch, many appear to remain relevant today. If I had to make a recommendation now it would not be for research into technical matters but rather as to whether the present arrangements for water research are the best that could be devised (though of course I appreciate that any conclusion would be an opinion).

Also around 1986 I gladly accepted an invitation from Arthur Boon then still at WRc to join him in preparation of a section in a volume entitled *Comprehensive Biotechnology* to be published by Pergamon Press and dealing with 'The Principles, Applications and Regulation of Biotechnology in Industry, Agriculture and Medicine'. Our contribution was a review of 'High Intensity Systems in Activated-Sludge Processes'. Looking at the text again after some 14 years I feel sure that I remember correctly that Arthur contributed most of the paper because I had only very limited experience of several of the newer devices described therein; however he courteously put my name before his after the title. It was indeed a pleasure to renew the collaboration we had had over many years at WPRL.

Aside from business I frequently took part in golf days the firm held in the Autumn at the very pleasant course at Tandridge near Oxted; and after a while a Spring Meeting was introduced, and was held on various courses, not far from Redhill. Additionally from time to time we had a match between the so-called 'clean water Partners' and the 'dirty water' ones. Representing the former were usually Richard

51. Nick Dawes and I celebrating at Tandridge Golf Club.

Phillips and Bill Carlyle and the latter were myself and originally Peter Norris, and after his retirement Nick Dawes. Results were fairly evenly divided but Plate 51 shows Nick Dawes and myself on one occasion at Tandridge when we won, drinking champagne kindly provided by Ted Flaxman.

CHAPTER 7

Private Practice as a Consultant: 1986-96

IN 1986 I BECAME 60 and thus eligible to draw my 'frozen' Civil
Service Pension. Coincidentally the Partnership decided that
because London rents had become excessively high we would move
our offices from Victoria Street to Redhill in Surrey. I did not feel I
could travel from home to Redhill every day, and certainly did not
want to move from our present house, so I resigned from the
Partnership to become a Consultant to the firm. One of the
consequences of this was that to continue to be taxed as a self-
employed person I had to work for at least one other client. As a result
I undertook a number of 'freelance' projects (mentioned later).

In 1986 I co-authored a paper with Mr C J (Colin) Appleyard and
Dr G R (Ray) Groves, dealing with 'Treatment and Disposal of
Industrial Wastewaters'. The paper was presented at a Conference
entitled 'World Water '86', organized by the Institution of Civil
Engineers. The opening address was given by HRH The Princess
Anne. The paper contained accounts of several treatability studies the
firm had made at overseas sites in Dali City, China, Jubail in Saudi
Arabia, Perth in Western Australia and near Fresno in California. Each
of these projects had interesting, even unique, features but I deal with
these in my subsequent accounts of experiences in individual
countries. In passing I note that I have not previously mentioned that
Colin Appleyard is a leading expert on industrial effluent treatment
who joined the firm in the late seventies after working for several
years with Bostock, Hill and Rigby, a firm specializing in this field. I
have many happy memories of working with Colin in the UK, RSA
and Delft. He originally lived not far away from Kath and me in

Hitchin but then moved to be nearer the firm's HQ in Redhill (where if memory serves he was for a time a Partner). Since then I have regrettably lost touch with him, though I learned quite recently that he is now living in France. Dr Ray Groves worked for a time alongside Colin in our RSA firm, headed by Rodney Squires, and subsequently worked with Rodney in California and elsewhere in the development of cross-flow microfiltration.

At around the time of my change to Consultant status I had an interesting involvement in assessment of a new method for treatment of wastewaters by so-called Root-Zone technology. This treatment was devised by Professor Kickuth, a soil microbiologist from Kassel University in Germany. It consisted in passing the wastewater by horizontal flow through a shallow bed of soil implanted with reeds (Phragmites). At appropriate hydraulic loadings the growth and decay of the root system produced sufficient interstices to ensure that the wastewater would flow through the soil and, as Kickuth argued, a much wider spectrum of micro-organisms present in the soil than develops in conventional biological treatment plants metabolised the biodegradable impurities. At the invitation of a small firm that had been established in the UK to promote the technology, Oceans International Services Limited (later Root Zone Limited (RZL)), I went via Hanover (Germany) to meet the Professor near Kassel and see some of the plants that were operating there. A particularly impressive one had been treating effluent from a large textile factory at Windelsbleiche to a high standard for quite some time. Plate 23 shows the edge of one of the reed beds. I came back thinking that the method had some potential, at least for small flows or where large areas of land were available. As it happened our firm was appointed in collaboration with RZL to design and supervise the construction of a sewage treatment plant for a small community in Holtby, Yorkshire. Several other plants were subsequently brought into operation in the UK by Regional Water Authorities in some cases for 'effluent polishing' rather than as the main means of treatment. I think this reflects limitations imposed by the inherent resistance to flow imposed by beds of soil and it seemed to me that modifications such as were introduced' particularly in the USA, where reeds were implanted into beds of gravel or gravel plus soil offered the best prospects for further development. For a short period I undertook to act as a consultant to RZL though I don't recall ever working in that capacity. I have long since lost touch with subsequent developments so I have nothing to recall about more recent history.

Towards the end of 1987 I delivered a paper on Quality Objectives and Standards to an international conference on Environmental Protection of the North Sea organized by WRc and held at the International Maritime Organisation (IMO) in London. My paper dealt in some detail with the technical issues. However in a somewhat jocular attempt to put the scale of pollution arising from sewage outfalls into perspective I put up a slide showing the North Sea with just a dot in the middle. I explained that the dot was not a fly that had settled on the screen but a realistic attempt to show the area occupied by the sum of the mixing zones around all the submarine outfalls from the UK. I recall that after the conference I received a nice letter from Mike Rouse of WRc thanking me for my contribution. Mike had succeeded John Van der Post as Director and Chief Executive at the Centre. He went on to become DoE's Chief Drinking Water Inspector in which post he was awarded a CBE. Currently he is President of the International Water Association (IWA). Incidentally one of his senior staff at DoE was my former colleague at B & P, Claire Jackson, who had retired from the practice when the firm moved to Redhill.

Two of my freelance projects came from the Hydraulics Research Laboratory (HRL) at Wallingford. The first of these required me to comment on the assessments HRL had made of the effects on water quality likely to result from introduction of a half-tide barrage (one that was closed in the middle of the ebb tide) into the River Lagan in Northern Ireland. The object of the barrage was to ensure that the then existing unsightly mud flats were covered and rowing would be possible at all states of the tide. Though I cannot recall the detail of my conclusions I know they were favourable. The barrage was subsequently built and so far as I am aware has operated successfully ever since.

The second of my HRL projects was to review the water quality aspect of the impressive and extensive work that Nick Odd and his team had done to develop models for forecasting the effects of the introduction of a proposed barrage into the Tees Estuary as part of an urban renewal project promoted by the Teeside Development Corporation.

My opinion, after reviewing 18 reports on various individual aspects, was that although the water quality model required further 'tuning' to yield predictions as accurate as would ideally be desirable, the initial predictions obtained with it could reasonably be regarded as reliable in a qualitative sense, and certainly represented a remarkable achievement having regard to the limited time available to develop it and the very considerable complexity of the vertically stratified estuarine regime. Broad indications were that the barrage would improve water quality upstream of its location and if there were deteriorations downstream they would be small and in particular not sufficient to alter the suitability of the water for its existing uses.

To proceed with the proposal required introduction of a Parliamentary Bill and Nick Odd had to respond to substantial questioning by a House of Lords Committee. However the Committee accepted HRL's forecasts, the Bill proceeded and the barrage was built. So far as I am aware it has proved satisfactory.

Then in 1987 George Eden and I presented another paper this time to an IPHE Symposium in London on Water Quality and Health. We gave our views on the Benefits and Costs of EEC Legislation on Water Quality.

Among other projects in which I became involved after I had resigned from Partnership included:

- provision of advice on assessment of the likely influence on water quality of changes in the geometry and hydraulic regime of Lake Trawsfynydd, analysis of the water from which had been, as I have noted earlier, one of my first assignments about 50 years previously;
- analysis of data obtained from bacterial tracer studies for siting a marine outfall at Charmouth in Dorset; and
- advising an industrial client on treatability studies and process design for a plant for purifying pharmaceutical waste.

I don't remember much about other UK activities prior to 1990 except than that in 1988, as part of my responsibilities as the Consultants' representative on the WRc Council, I wrote a long letter to the Hon. Colin Moynihan, DoE's Parliamentary Under Secretary at the time. This set out our concerns that following privatisation of the Centre we would no longer have access to much of the Centre's research, most of which would hitherto be carried out under contract for the new water Plc's. My impression is that this went down like a 'lead balloon'.

Then I think around 1990 George Eden and I, again 'freelancing', undertook a study for DoE to advise on the future of the Department's Standing Committee of Analysts following privatization of the water industry and creation of WRc. This involved taking the views of a wide range of organizations who either conducted analysis or made use of analytical results; many of their executives were, of course, old colleagues or people we knew well from our professional contacts with them. An obvious conclusion might well have been that responsibility should be transferred to the newly formed WRc. However we were by no means certain at that stage how WRc would evolve and because the Committee had an excellent reputation and was guided by an experienced DoE analytical expert, Albert Goodman, we thought it prudent to recommend that it should remain with DoE at least until the role of WRc became clearer. I believe that is what happened but I have lost touch with subsequent developments.

Around this time I got a call from Wes Eckenfelder in which he asked whether I knew of a UK firm that might like to associate with his firm (Eckenfelder Inc based in Nashville) in collaborative projects. My first thought of course was 'What about B & P?' After consultation with Partners this idea was given the 'green light' and an association was forged. The immediate consequence for me was that the involvement I had had with Wes in giving lectures in the courses he organized at IAWPRC conferences was extended and we gave an Eckenfelder-Binnie course for overseas participants at one of the hotels near Gatwick airport. I continued to provide an input into the conference courses until one in Vancouver in 1998. Prior to that one I had started to suffer from angina and additionally I had retired from private practice two years previously, not least because I had begun to feel I was getting too much out of touch with the latest developments. So I asked Wes to (using an American expression) 'include me out' and proffered my apologies.

Also in 1990 I recall answering questions about pollution of beaches put to me by members of a House of Commons Environmental Committee, in a room within the Parliament building. I think I was among the last few to give evidence and I got the impression that the Committee had the situation well into focus; certainly nothing controversial arose.

Then again in 1990 I was very pleased to receive unexpectedly an invitation from Sir Eldon Griffiths to attend a dinner party to welcome the Director General (Mr Liu) of a then recently formed British-Taiwan Institute and his wife together with a Taiwanese delegation. Mr Liu was also the Representative of the Pacific Cultural Foundation which had been for many years developing contacts between Taiwanese cultural organisations and those in the USA and other Pacific Rim countries. It was an altogether pleasurable event especially coming not long after my visit to Taiwan (see later).

Also as part of my 'freelance' activities I gave advice in 1990 to the Test and Itchen Angling Association on apparent deteriorations in water quality in the rivers. However, if memory serves, I attributed these deteriorations as being largely due to reduced flows pertaining in the relative dry conditions of the period.

In the same year Wes Eckenfelder and I were each simultaneously awarded the IAWPRC's Karl Imhoff – Pierre Koch (two respected early pioneers) Medal for research that had had an impact on full-scale practice. I remember we received the medals at a meeting abroad, at which they were presented to us by the late Professor Poul Harremoës, the then current President of IAWPRC, shown in the photograph (Plate 24). I had had many pleasant meetings with Poul and was greatly saddened to learn of his recent death at a relatively early age. Also in the following year I advised on water quality implications for a proposed Broad Oak Reservoir.

Among his many other accomplishments our former Senior Partner G M (Geoffrey) Binnie was a Fellow of the Royal Society (FRS) and a year or two after I joined the Partnership he put my name forward for election (with as co-sponsor, I believe, Sir Edward Boyle). However I did not get elected. Geoffrey was kind enough to say that because I had worked in a field that was much under-appreciated not many of his fellow members knew of me. Then a few years later the then Senior Partner, Mr R T (Ronald) Gerrard, in conjunction I believe with the late Mr D A D Reeve, the Chief Executive of the Severn-Trent Water Authority, very kindly proposed me for Fellowship of the then Academy of Engineering. This soon after became the Royal Academy of Engineering, a body that has become in effect the engineering analogue of the Royal Society, albeit a few centuries younger. I was delighted when in 1991 this proposal was accepted and I have much enjoyed all the RA Eng events in which I have been involved, especially as they have enabled me to meet old friends whom I otherwise might not have seen, such as Professor Michael Hamlin (formerly Principal and Vice Chancellor, University of

Dundee) and Professor Peter Wolf, Emeritus Professor of the City University, London. Peter, of course, has kindly provided the Foreword to these Memoirs.

Then from looking through old records I came across a paper I had drafted around 1990 giving an account of some of the work I had done as part of the firm's project to identify the best means of uprating Severn-Trent Water's (STW) water treatment plant at Strensham. The work concentrated on the removal of ammonia by nitrification in upward flow sludge-blanket clarifiers. Looking at the draft now the data and the conclusions I drew from it seem quite interesting. However it appears I never submitted it for publication even though the draft indicates I had STW's permission. I am at a loss to recall why I did not. Possibly I may have thought that some of my conclusions were too speculative or there may have been some political obstacle that I have now forgotten.

My last two professional activities in the UK, as consultant to the firm, both involved collaboration with Paul Cooper of WRc, who had joined WPRL not long before my move into private practice. One simply involved revision and updating of a chapter I had prepared a year or two earlier for the book (which I refer to elsewhere) by Wes Eckenfelder on waste treatment technology. The other was an account of the history of development of the AS process for an International Conference later held in Manchester. In both cases Paul and I were co-authors. Again, as so often, my recollections of the latter event are coloured by non-technical irrelevancies, in this case, of being taken with other delegates to the set (or perhaps 'site' would be more appropriate) of the famous television soap 'Coronation Street'. All very interesting but since I don't normally watch the programme I was unable to relate what I saw to events on screen.

CHAPTER 8

Overseas Work in Private Practice

Peru

SOON AFTER joining the Partnership I was asked to go to Lima to assist in a World Bank funded project to prepare a scheme for conveying water from the River Mantaro to Lima to augment the supply to the city. By coincidence our former Senior Partner Geoffrey Binnie, FRS, travelled on the same flight, though he was going to supervise another project. My role was to examine the effect of wastewaters from the mining of copper, zinc and lead at Cerro de Pasco on the quality of water in the Mantaro and advise on what might be necessary to prevent unacceptable impact. The mines were located around the headwaters of the river at an altitude of about 14,000 feet (4230m) but could be reached by road from Lima within about half a day. Before leaving I had been medically examined and told that there were no overt indications of a significant risk of developing altitude sickness at 14,000 feet, although a precise prediction of how I would react was not possible. I went up with several relatively young engineers, our party travelling in two jeeps. As it turned out by the time we had reached 10,000 feet I felt distinctly 'woozy'; and at 14,000 feet I could hardly drag one foot in front of the other. Fortunately the US firm that had developed the mines had installed a small hospital and I was escorted in by two of the young engineers, one on each shoulder. I was examined by a doctor who put a stethoscope on my chest and after a moment said, 'Ah, crepitation!' I concluded from this that fluid had accumulated in my lungs. Had I realized then that one of the more acute symptoms of mountain sickness could be 'water on the brain' I would have been much more

120

worried than I was at the time. I should add that this was not the main reason for adopting the phrase as the title of these Memoirs – and in that connection Kathy said it would have been just as relevant to make the title 'Water Down the Drain'! At the hospital they gave me a tranquillizer, put me to bed and connected me to an oxygen supply. I stayed in bed for about two days during which I was told that my body would have manufactured more haemoglobin. I certainly felt much better and for the next three or four days of the trip I was able to work at about half pace, examining the mining activities and sources of wastewater. Plates 25 and 26 show some of the mine buildings. The operations were quite conventional with the spent originally metal bearing sulphidic ores being deposited in tailings ponds from which the overflows plus additional wastes from the extraction of copper and so-called acid mine waters were released to the Mantaro. These acid mine waters were derived from the bacterial oxidation of sulphides to sulphuric acid.

Among features that surprised me was the fact that some of the dried out tailings ponds had been converted into football pitches; and, so I was told, the Americans had created some sort of golf course nearby (I had hoped to be able to see how far my drives went at the high altitudes (shades of the moon landing) but regrettably I never saw the course).

The release of the wastewaters to the Mantaro had caused the river in the vicinity of the outfalls, and someway downstream, to turn orange in colour, this being mainly a consequence of the oxidation and precipitation of the dissolved iron from the acid mine waters as ferric salts. To what extent any undesirable impurities would have remained in solution by the time the water had passed on its long route, taking in at least one lake, was not clear at this point, but I concluded that conventional treatment of the wastewaters at the mining site plus further treatment of the water before release to the distribution system could have comfortably eliminated any problem.

I made another visit a few years later to identify factors affecting water quality in rivers flowing to Lima including the R Rimac. I think it was probably on this visit that I went swimming on one of the beaches near Lima with James Hetherington and later joined James and his wife Elizabeth for lunch. James was in charge of our operations in Peru at the time and became a Partner in our UK HQ a few years later. On the day of our outing the sky seemed quite grey and overcast and although I was aware that we were near the Equator I was amazed to find just a few hours later that I was quite red and sore with sunburn.

Australia

Soon after joining B & P I felt that as I had made many contacts during my tour in 1970 some prospecting in Australia would make sense. I began by submitting a paper on recent developments in the UK on treatment and disposal of sewage sludge to the Australian Water and Wastewater Association's (AWWA) 6th Federal Convention, Melbourne (May 1974). Then in the following year as one of the principal lecturers I gave a series of 5 papers in the AWWA's Summer School in Canberra. A little earlier B & P had set up a local firm, Binnie International (Australia) Pty, with offices in William Street, Melbourne, with David Cowie, Tom Hammond and myself as Directors. By good fortune I then got our local firm appointed by the New South Wales State Pollution Control Commission to develop a monitoring programme for the State's major rivers. I recall that myself and an Australian counterpart had a flight over the area in a small plane (Plate 27) and also a boat trip from the George River into Botany Bay to get the scale of the task into perspective. The project went well until the very last moment (in 1976) when due to an unexpected printing problem I failed by a day or two to get my quite bulky report to the Secretary of the Commission by a 'deadline' arising from his departure on an overseas trip. I think I was forgiven and the report was well received but yet another embarrassing moment still lingers in my memory.

Towards the end of 1976 the Department of Housing and Construction in Canberra invited our local firm to compete for a major project, to advise on the extent of need to meet low limits for the content of N and P in the Canberra sewage treatment plant. The Canberra plant was, in its day, among the most advanced in the world, having been designed in a similar style to certain plants in California to remove phosphorus by chemical precipitation and nitrogen in a biological denitrification unit 'fuelled' by methanol, in addition to attainment of the conventional aims of eliminating the majority of organics and suspended matter. The original aim was to protect the River Molonglo into which the plant effluent was released and Lake Burrinjuck, into which the Molonglo flowed, from the effect of pollution, especially unwanted growths of algae. It transpires from what we learned later that in our offer I gave a rather downbeat appraisal of what might be achieved in the time and with the resources I proposed be deployed, whereas our competitors apparently produced much more grandiloquently optimistic proposals. I think our clients must have judged that I was 'speaking with the voice of experience' and we were awarded the project, the largest gained by our Australian firm up to that time. It proved a very interesting one lasting nearly 8 months. I fielded a team of about six including myself, all from our B & P headquarters in the UK, plus for specialist advice, John Lund FRS, an expert in algology, from the Freshwater Biological Association at Windermere, whom I knew well from that connection. In our Report to the National Capital Development Commission and the Department of Construction we concluded that of the two algal nutrients N and P elimination of phosphorus alone should suffice to prevent algal nuisance so the extra expense (around 300 000 A$ per year) of removing N could be avoided. I'm afraid I have lost touch with developments since the project was completed though I have heard nothing to suggest that our conclusions were incorrect. Mr D A (Dave) Henley, from the Department of Housing and Construction, and I gave an introductory paper about the study to the seventh

AWWA Federal Convention in 1977; and then in 1979 during the IWPC conference at which I became President as I mentioned earlier Dave, David Keiller and I gave a joint paper describing the findings of the study in detail.

Because we gained other projects in Australia and also New Zealand I found myself it seemed almost continually jet lagged. Indeed in one year around about 1976 I went from London to Australia five times. On one of my trips my Partners very generously proposed that I should take Kath with me (at the firm's expense) and on that trip which for me extended about nine weeks Kath was with me for about six of them. I suppose mainly because in those days we flew 1st class she had the enjoyable experience on a flight from Melbourne to Sydney of being invited into the pilot's cabin and being allowed to remain there throughout the landing. In the early stages of the visit we attended the 1976 IAWPR Conference at Sydney which included an opening ceremony in the Sydney Opera House, and meeting during the proceedings a number of senior politicians including Neville Wran, the New South Wales State Governor.

While in Sydney we were also taken to a horse-race meeting at Randwick. We backed the winner of the first race but shortly after it finished there was a torrential rainstorm and the remainder of the meeting was abandoned. 'Never mind,' said our hosts, 'You can bet on the Melbourne races', which were being shown on CCTV. I was amazed how comfortable the whole set-up was compared with my experiences at the few race meetings I had attended as a young man in the UK. In contrast to standing around outside in sometimes cold weather placing my bets directly with bookies, at Randwick we sat very comfortably behind huge plate glass windows and had our bets placed and winnings if any returned by a staff of attractive young ladies.

I remember that we also went together to Canberra where, driving a borrowed Volkswagen, with one of my typical gaffes I turned in the wrong direction into a one-way street. We had to stay stock still while what seemed like a six-lane cavalcade of vehicles flowed past us. Also from Canberra we had a boat trip down the Molonglo and into Lake Burrinjuck just after some severe storms and consequent flooding. The amount of floating debris in the lake had to be seen to be believed.

Another memory of the trip on the eastern side of Australia was the occurrence when we were in Melbourne of a total eclipse of the sun around midday. I was at a technical forum and while able to see the eclipse through the window was able simultaneously to watch a TV programme showing the event as seen from the country's chief meteorological station in South Australia.

Before she returned independently to the UK, Kath came with me for a week or two to Perth where our local firm had started on the first of several projects for which we had been appointed. One of these was a fascinating assignment to prepare an Environmental Impact Statement for a new uranium mine that the Western Mining Company was proposing to open at Yeelirrie, about 400 km northeast of Perth in the Western Australian desert. Although I had worked in the radiochemical field, as mentioned earlier, and we had arranged to have the assistance of a senior member of the UK's National Radiological Protection Board, M C (Mike) O'Riordan, Western Mining said at the start of the project, 'Although you guys have a great deal of relevant expertise you don't actually know anything about uranium mining, do you?' We had to admit that we didn't so W M said, 'Well we've arranged for you to go on a tour of uranium mines in the USA.' As a result I flew to Albuquerque went on to Denver and had a fascinating tour of US mines (Plate 28), including the Lucky Mac mine in Utah. We had a brief stop en route back to LA at Salt Lake City. There we listened to a service in the Mormon temple where the acoustics were said to be so good that you could 'hear a pin drop'; I can almost believe it.

On return to Perth we flew to the site in a small aircraft and were immediately struck by the remoteness of the location. Plate 29 shows some of the trial open cast workings. The thought also came to mind that if, after the uranium ore had been removed, a site for disposal of nuclear waste were wanted the mined area would be a good choice.

Assessment of the likely environmental impact or, to make a slightly superficial summary, the lack of it, was broadly straightforward though some of our estimates, especially for example of the release of radon and radon daughter products to the air, were inevitably to some extent hypothetical. A few months after we had finished our work Mike O'Riordan delivered a paper on 'Source Terms for Airborne Radioactivity arising from uranium mill wastes', in which he kindly included me as a co-author, to an OECD Nuclear Energy Agency Seminar in 1979 in Canada.

While in Perth I worked in collaboration with Geoff Fernie who was the local Partner of Maunsell and Partners. Geoff and his charming wife were very hospitable and among other things took me to play golf with them at their local course near the coast south of the city; and also to dine at a splendid restaurant called the Yum-Yum Tree, named essentially because there was indeed a tree growing almost it seemed out through the roof of the building. Another memory of Perth is watching the MCC touring team attempting to cope with Dennis Lillee when he was bowling flat out at the WACA ground, which has one of the fastest wickets in the country; and watching 'on the box', with Geoff Fernie, Derek Randall's splendid attempt to win the Centennial Test for the MCC in Melbourne. The locals on the popular side of the ground, as it happened quite close to the police station, were apt to crash their empty beer cans together in time with Lillee's footsteps. Someone told me that they also used to shout, 'Kill, kill...' synchronously but I never heard that.

I think it was also around this time when in one of the main Australian papers there was the headline 'Outlook bleak, more Snow'. This, of course, was a reference to the England fast bowler John Snow who had taken a stack of Australian wickets in the previous Test Match.

Golf games in Perth were just some of the many I have enjoyed in

Australia. One that particularly sticks in my memory was playing in a competition on a Sydney course on the occasion of an International Conference (probably the 1976 IAWPR one). At the subsequent prize-giving ceremony all of a sudden to my surprise my name was called out. I went up to the presenter of the prizes saying, 'I'm surprised to be called because I didn't think I'd been playing very well.' 'You're right,' he said, 'but we had a prize for the best score by an overseas competitor and you were the only one!'

I remember also playing in a fourball on one of the Sydney courses and all four of us hit reasonable drives on to the fairway or light rough but by the time we reached where the balls appeared to have fallen we could find only one. Apparently the others had been removed by large crows that we had seen circling the area – an incident that parallels a well documented one at I think the South Herts Golf Club where the late Dai Rees was a professional.

Among other enjoyable times was staying as I usually did when in Melbourne at the Windsor Hotel, which in styling (at the time) could be described as traditionally English with splendidly large leather armchairs in the spacious ground floor lounge. On one occasion fellow guests were John Thaw and Sheila Hancock who were playing at the local theatre about two or three blocks away.

At around this time I made contact again with Roy Marsh and his charming first wife, Joy. Roy had been spending a year in Australia monitoring the Dunlop Rubber Company's operations there and in other parts of the South Pacific. We had some good dinners together particularly at Glo-Glo's restaurant just north of the city. Very sadly Joy died comparatively young from cancer. Roy has since remarried and is living happily with his delightful and very talented second wife, Linda, in their most attractive home near Haywards Heath.

Another project in Australia took me again to Tasmania, this time to assess the impact of pollution mainly arising from Launceston on water quality in the River Tamar. I seem to recall that we did a little preliminary crude modelling to reconcile observed quality characteristics with the polluting loads. However a somewhat clearer memory (again as usual non-technical) is of a trip downriver by launch. This afforded me a view of a bridge designed by Maunsell & Partners which to me looked very elegant but rather unusual in structure (Plate 30); and what seemed the epitome of a Devonshire cream tea, of the sort one might have had in the Tamar Valley in the UK, except that we had it at about 11 o'clock in the morning.

Then I think it must have been around 1978 David Cowie and I went to the Gold Coast council's offices to offer services for the design of a new wastewater treatment plant for the city. I was outlining our proposals and said something along the lines of 'and the rationale for this course of action is …'. At that one of the council members broke in with, 'Who is this geezer and what's he on about with his rations?' This didn't altogether attract me to the idea of pursuing the project but a few months later fate took a hand in that the council was sacked, for corruption I was told.

In 1979 not long after this incident I gave a series of 9 lectures in a training course organized by P F (Philip) Greenfield of the Department of Chemical Engineering, University of Queensland. This took place at Surfers Paradise. If memory serves Philip Greenfield had also been involved in the organization of the course I took part in at Palmerston North in New Zealand. As usual I now remember little of the proceedings and looking at the 270 pages of Volume 2 of the course notes, which contains the texts of my lectures, I am once again somewhat shocked by the difference between what I seemed to know something about then and what I comprehend now.

Around about 1980 my Partner Ted Flaxman obtained a major project to design a scheme for disposal of the wastewaters from Perth. In this he examined three main options: treatment on land and disposal thereon; advanced treatment and release to a partially enclosed bay (Owen Anchorage); and primary treatment followed by discharge to deep ocean waters. My involvement in the project was limited to a very brief review of the results of some of the studies of dispersion using bacterial tracers though Colin Appleyard did some substantial work to assess the facilities necessary and associated costs of dealing with the industrial wastewaters. The last of the three options proved to be the preferred choice. I found this particularly pleasing, in view of the strong Australian regard for protection of the environment and participation in bathing and other water sports; and also because of the work that Ted, our former partner, Peter Norris, and myself had done over the years to try to ensure rational attitudes to marine disposal. I was especially pleased when a year or two later Ted's project won an environmental award.

Also in 1980 in conjunction with K R (Ken) Brendish I presented a paper on 'Developments in Liquid Waste Treatment Technology' to a meeting of the Institution of Engineers, Australia. The paper, subsequently published in the IEM Transactions, was about treatment of industrial wastewaters. Ken Brendish had been one of my former colleagues at WPRL before forming his own firm and then subsequently joining B & P.

I also got involved a year or two later in advising on the control of odour arising from the sludge drying beds at Melbourne's then newest and quite advanced sewage treatment plant. Regretfully for the life of me I cannot now remember what the substance of my advice was.

If memory serves my last visit to Australia was in 1983, when I presented a paper on 'Protection of natural waters from the effects of excessive enrichment – development models' at the 10th AWWA Federation Convention in Sydney. The models I considered were essentially somewhat speculative attempts to relate algal growth in a river, a lake and an estuary to nutrient loadings. The lake in this case was Lough Neagh in Northern Ireland. In the paper I offered forecasts of the effects of local plans to reduce the phosphorus loadings on the lake on its algal content from the then present date 1983 until the year 2000. I would be intrigued to know what actually happened but have not subsequently been in a position to find out.

I would very much have liked to return to Australia but by 1983 my

commitments had become focussed on other areas. One of these was
China, though as it happened one of my main assignments there was,
as I record later, as a member of a team led by Mike Oddie from our
Australian firm and mainly staffed by his colleagues.

China

Between 1982 and 1992 I went on business to China 15 times. My
first visit was in the category of what my colleagues described at the
time as 'casting bread on the water'. By that I mean that at the
Partnership's expense I responded to invitations to lecture on
pollution control in both Beijing and Shanghai, spending two or three
days in both cities. The following events seem to indicate that in this
case the effort paid off. The circumstances were that in 1983 a major
MasterPlan study was launched to determine the best means of
disposing of the wastewaters from Shanghai so that new water quality
standards set for the Huangpu River that flows through Shanghai, and
which received most of the city's effluent, could be met. The
condition of the River at this time had become so bad that the local
authorities had developed what was called an 'index of stink' and in
1982 there were no fewer than 150 'black stink days'.

Our Australian firm, which drew on our UK personnel in
appropriate circumstances, was one of several invited to submit an
offer to carry out the study. A senior Chinese contact told me that
when they were looking through the offers and the lists of people who
would be involved from the various firms the only name they
recognized, because of my previous visit, was mine, so they chose our
firm. I suppose one could say that the philosophy of 'better the devil
you know' may have resulted in our Australian firm being appointed –
but how true all that is I cannot be certain.

As a consequence of our Australian firm being appointed I
remember that on my first visit to discuss our task with the client I
travelled on an Australian Diplomatic Passport. Heading our team was
Mike Oddie who, if memory serves, was English in origin but after

working for the UK firm on several overseas projects then emigrated to Australia. I initially worked mainly with Julian Summers, a talented young environmental engineer from our Australian firm. We stayed in a small hotel near the bridge at the mouth of Suzhou Creek (shown in Plate 31), which was heavily polluted especially with industrial effluents. Fairly near within the city was a shop selling excellent Chinese rugs and carpets, and I bought a pair of rugs. The shop arranged transport to the UK. Though this took several months they ultimately arrived safe and sound and have lain in our living room ever since with absolutely no sign of wear.

In my ignorance in my early visit I was quite surprised in both Shanghai and Beijing to find on occasions taxi drivers playing western classical music on their car tape decks. On the other side of the coin as it were I spent a very enjoyable evening at the concert hall in Shanghai attending a performance of a Chinese violin concerto, the Butterfly Lovers, which has an intriguing blend of western-sounding and Chinese music. By good fortune in one of the Beijing airport shops prior to departure back to the UK I spotted and bought a tape of the score which I still play from time to time at home.

The Shanghai project itself was particularly interesting to me because the Huangpu (Plate 32) was about the same size as the Thames and its water quality was almost uniform with respect to depth and width, variations in quality being essentially longitudinal. I therefore concluded that we could develop a 1-D model of the same style as that for the Thames, though using the concept I had evolved earlier envisaging the river being composed of a chain of uniformly mixed segments. Accordingly Julian Summers and I began by doing just that and then Julian went on to use in addition other models that the Chinese had acquired from the USA. To cut a long story short we obtained acceptably good agreement between observed distributions of DO and other quality characteristics and those predicted from the polluting loads, provided that in the case of DO instead of using a mass-transfer coefficient for absorption of atmospheric oxygen of around 5.5 cm/h, the figure determined for the Thames, we assumed instead a figure of 7 cm/h for the Huangpu. We considered that this higher figure was the possible result of the very much greater disturbance of the water by shipping. Using the model together with estimates made by Colin Appleyard on the costs of treating industrial effluents at source the team concluded that to treat Shanghai's wastewaters sufficiently for their release directly into the Huangpu without contravention of the PRC water quality standards the cost would be around US $1300 million. In contrast their collection and discharge by pipeline terminating well offshore in the R Chiangjiang (the Yangtze) would be less than half that figure.

In several visits to Shanghai I stayed in different hotels. In one of these the hotel was of an older traditional style, located just across the road from what had formerly been the French Club. This was remarkably well equipped with two restaurants, four billiard tables (one without pockets for some game that I presume was based on getting cannons), ten-pin bowling, table tennis and more besides. As a consequence in the evening after work Mike Oddie, Colin Appleyard and I usually with other team members used to go over to enjoy the facilities.

In my last visit in connection with the project we met in Beijing to iron out one or two slightly controversial difficulties regarding the final choice of option with our PRC counterparts. I was more than pleased when it was resolved to adopt the scheme to discharge into the Chiangjiang. On this occasion we stayed in one of the latest up-market hotels which was at least the equal of the best that I have stayed in elsewhere. Its facilities included several restaurants and bars, a delightful large foyer where a Chinese lady pianist regularly performed, a pool table in one of the bars and in a separate small building 3 snooker tables. Mike Oddie and I had several frames of snooker and on one occasion we were quite pleased with ourselves when we beat some Americans staying in the hotel at their game, Pool, in the bar room of the hotel.

I think it was not long after the Shanghai project began that I was appointed by the UK's Overseas Development Agency (ODA) to assess the scope for an ODA funded Sino-British pollution control project to assist the Chongqing Institute of Environmental Science and Monitoring to develop a plan for controlling pollution in the River Chiangjiang. The city is located on the Chiangjiang some distance upstream of the Three Gorges region (which of course is the site of the current huge dam project). I was accompanied on the visit by our firm's training officer, Mr R G (Rodney) Amster. We had contacts with a host of local Chinese professionals but primarily with the Chongqing Institute of Environmental Science and Monitoring (CIESM). We concluded that the effort required to produce what the Chinese wanted, which in effect was virtually a complete master plan, would cost far more than the available ODA funds. We recommended instead that attention be focussed on defining the prospects for developing a water quality model and relevant training of Chinese personnel.

On returning from Chongqing with Rodney Ampster we were met in the early evening at Beijing airport by two young Chinese ladies from a Science and Technology liaison unit who said they were going to take us to a traditional Peking Duck restaurant where we would get dinner. On the journey by car one of them asked whether I had a family. Without thinking I said, 'Yes, a wife and daughter and two dogs.' (Plates 33 and 34). This induced some laughter from them and then, of course, I remembered that in parts of China (it is alleged) they still eat dogs. When we reached the restaurant Rodney and I ordered Peking Duck for the four of us only to find that the two young ladies had, they said, already eaten. Well we didn't want to see half the food wasted so we started to eat. The girls busied themselves with wrapping duck, laden with sauce, in pancakes and passing these to us as soon as we had finished the preceding one but it was rather like being on the end of an inexorable factory production line and we finally left having considerably overeaten.

Some time later the firm was appointed by ODA to carry out the type of study we had recommended earlier – but with attention to be focussed on the measures needed locally to meet recently introduced PRC standards for the Chiangjiang. I recall (I hope correctly) going on the project with, to cover modelling, David Keiller, and if memory serves Daniel Yang, an environmental engineer from our Hong Kong firm. Plate 35 shows our party on the River, with Chinese counterparts and some of their family members. There was a clear need to purify the many industrial and domestic wastewaters which could be seen cascading into the River down its gorge-like banks at the very least to meet the standards in the immediate vicinity of their points of entry or alternatively to permit defined mixing zones. The flow of the River is so huge, however, (averaging around 20000 m³/s) that not far downstream their impact was hardly detectable. However we soon established that a major difficulty, if standards were to be maintained, would arise because for about 8 quality characteristics the standards were exceeded in the water entering the area from upstream. What if anything was subsequently done about that I have not heard.

In March 1984 I gave yet another paper on industrial effluent treatment at an 'International Symposium on Waste Water Engineering and Management' in Guanzhou (a popular tourist centre) organized jointly by the Hong Kong Polytechnic and the Society of Environmental Science of Guangdong. I had a difficult and unduly lengthy journey back to HK, the delays from which caused me to miss my original connection for a flight to Kuala Lumpur. My visit there was to present the opening address at a conference, which I mention again in my account of activities in Malaysia. After an overnight stop I then endeavoured to get a seat on a morning flight to KL only to find that it was fully booked. Fortunately one of the seats was occupied by an airline employee and when I explained that the conference I had to open was starting later in the day the airline (I think it must have been Cathay Pacific) kindly persuaded him to defer his journey until the next flight, so I made it to the conference just in time.

Then in November 1984 I was a member of a UK government sponsored team, led by Hugh (later Sir Hugh) Fish (chief Executive of Thames Water), that went to Beijing to conduct a China-UK Water Seminar in collaboration with a Chinese team led by Cheng Shengwu, Chairman of the Beijing Municipal Commission for Science and Technology, and including senior technical people from Beijing, Shanghai and Tianjiu. On that occasion I gave a paper on 'The Treatment and Disposal of Industrial Wastewaters'; and subsequently introduced a discussion session on 'Research and Development in Wastewater Treatment and Disposal'. The seminar went very well and I'm sure helped to promote UK trading interests in China. I was again accompanied on the visit by Daniel Yang. I had worked with Daniel on several projects and he spent quite some time with us in London polishing up his skills. He moved later from our HK firm into the Environmental Protection Department (EPD) and as I know from the cards we exchange at Christmas is still with them. Being a native of Hong Kong Daniel's principal languages were Cantonese and English but his Mandarin (the normal language in Beijing) was quite accomplished and this proved very useful for helping me in some of the discussion sessions.

About the time around 1986 that the firm moved its HQ and I resigned from the Partnership to become a consultant I directed an ODA project for the Chinese Government and Beijing Municipal Engineering Administration Division (BMEAD) 'to advise on the updating and improvement of the existing water quality monitoring system for the water supply from the Mi Yun reservoir in the Beijing Province'. This was one of three simultaneous projects involving members of the firm including Graham Thompson, a hydraulics expert who later became a Partner, and David Macdonald, with whom I had worked in Australia. Plate 36 shows the two of them with Chinese counterparts in the Forbidden City in Beijing.

The reservoir is a very large one the distance between its extremities being about 25 km and its capacity around 4 billion m^3. Plate 37 shows a BMEAD party monitoring water quality in the Reservoir. The quality of water in the feeder streams and in the reservoir itself was good but a feature attracting our attention was that the water was conveyed to a major treatment works in Beijing by an open canal around 100 km long. This had the disadvantage that in winter the water often froze at least at the surface; in summer the flow was also often restricted in this case by growths of algae; and the ready access of people to the canal and its nearness to a road rendered the water liable to pollution. Prior to our study BMEAD had already decided to install a pipe to replace the canal so our work which was broadly straightforward and carried out almost entirely by my colleagues focussed on our recommendations for improving water quality monitoring, data transmission and archiving of data; for strengthening the legislation providing for protection of the reservoir from pollution; exploiting the recreational potential of the reservoir and controlling its use for fish farming; and for training of local personnel in the various new analytical techniques we proposed should be adopted.

I think it may have been in connection with this project, or possibly in an independent one, that one of our instrument engineers, Alan George, and I gave talks and advice to Chinese counterparts on the design of monitoring schemes to protect water flowing (probably from Mi Yun) into the lakes adjoining the Summer and Winter Palaces in Beijing which were drawn on for potable supply. Plate 38 shows Alan and me with a Chinese lady counterpart. I particularly remember the project because one of the Chinese was, unusually, quite strident in expressing his views and was determined that we should recommend installation of a large battery of automatic quality monitors. I had considerable reservations about the justification for this because the commercially available monitors at that time needed careful 'nursing', but more importantly did not have the capability to measure several constituents of major importance. In the end I compromised by recommending installation of two units on the basis that, if nothing else, they would serve to give warning of major pollution of the watercourses and would provide basic training and experience in automatic quality monitoring on which the local staff could build.

In another project when either in Beijing or Shanghai I gave some brief technical advice to some people from far away Dali City in Yunnan province. Subsequently they appointed our UK firm to assist in developing a scheme for treatment of the wastewaters from the City, which included much heavy industry, especially pulp mills. These latter discharged 'black liquors' which together with the other industrial wastes and domestic sewage caused intense discolouration and foaming in the local river to which they were released. Without going into details, in the interests of brevity, local reasons indicated that it would be necessary to treat a mixture of the wastewaters without much of the normally desirable pre-treatment of those from industry at source.

The project was interesting in the slightly bizarre sense that because, through force of circumstances, we were unable to make the necessary treatability studies on site we had to have samples of the wastewaters flown back to our London laboratory. Moreover because of the costs these samples had to be small, their total volume being limited to 20 litres. This in turn meant that we had to use miniaturized versions of the test reactors that we would normally have used. Despite this we managed to establish that from a range of possibilities adequate treatment could be achieved using the activated-sludge process followed by chemical coagulation, although quantities of sludge generated would be excessive unless pre-treatment of some industrial effluents were introduced.

The Dali City project was just one of several that brought Chinese parties over to our Laboratory and involved enjoyable visits to Chinese restaurants including some of those in 'Little China' not far from Piccadilly Circus and also Ho's near Victoria Station. I also recall that I took one party to the Greenwich Observatory and being quite tickled when they insisted on being photographed with one foot on each side of the Greenwich Meridian.

Then around 1991 with several colleagues I became involved in work in support of an American University team engaged on a UNDTCD project to develop, for a North China Water Management Study (NCWM), a Macro-Economic Model for the large region that the study embraced. My Terms of Reference (TOR), which were quite unrealistic in my view, included furnishing the NCWM team with appropriate water quality models, demonstrating their applicability, developing effluent standards relevant to the condition of local rivers, estimating the benefits and costs of control actions and training of local counterpart staff in such activities.

My colleagues and I, perhaps through not being very familiar with economic modelling, were sceptical about what could reliably be achieved in the study, having regard to the massive data inputs we thought would be required and the relatively short time span allocated to the project. Moreover our scepticism also embodied doubts as to the extent the relevant Chinese administrators would act on the conclusions. However we did our best to furnish useful data.

My work was in two phases. In the first phase, largely a reconnaissance, I had concluded that a simple one-dimensional (1-D) model would probably suffice for forecasting the effects of changes in polluting loads on water quality in most of the rivers with adequate accuracy for broad planning purposes. In the second phase I worked for nearly a month in the offices of the Institute of Water Conservancy and Hydroelectric Power Research and in the nearby Centre for Water Quality Research (CWQR). Essentially all I could do was initiate the development of water quality models for the Luan He river in Hebai province and the Hu Tuo river in Shanxi province, make a preliminary demonstration of the use of the Luan He model for assessing costs of achieving desired water quality in the river, together with very approximate estimates of the costs of water pollution control in the region as a whole and in addition give some relevant training to the counterpart staff that I worked with in the CWQR. I remember causing the staff there some amusement when I started to call two of them who were prominent in helping me and both of whom had the same surname (Zhang) but different last names, No 1 and No 2. I suppose this might have been regarded as offensively patronizing but they seemed quite happy and indeed one of them, Zhang Min, actually identified himself as No 1,when a few years later he wrote asking me for my support, which I was delighted to give, for his applications to several US universities to enrol with them.

I think it was in the last phase of the study that I fell foul of one of the 'hazards' of dining in China. I went out on three successive nights with different groups of Chinese with whom I had worked on the study and other projects. The problem was that there is a traditional Chinese practice of toasting one's guests with a glass of Mautai, a liqueur which I should think has an alcohol content of nigh on 60% and which our UK team used cavalierly to term 'paint-stripper'. One is supposed to drain the glass in a gulp, turn it upside down to show that it has been drained, and utter the toast, 'Gambai!' Unfortunately I was usually heavily outnumbered by my hosts so when it came to the toasts individually they could take as few as they liked but I had to respond to at least the majority of them. I survived for two nights but on the third I was as 'sick as a dog' during the night and by morning I was in no condition to go to the airport to take the BA flight back to the UK. I had to phone and worry Kath with the news, that I would be delayed for a week because in those days the BA direct flights went only once a week. Fortunately as things turned out I was able to write the report required for the NCWM study in their offices rather than at home.

My last visit to China, around 1992, was to present a paper on 'Water Quality Modelling of Major River Systems' to a Seminar in Guangzou centring on improvement of the Pearl River Estuary environment. I find myself now slightly confused about this because I have in front of me a copy of a paper by me with the same title but dated 1998, two years after my retirement. I think the paper may not have been published originally but was later submitted to a further

Pearl River Conference by Graham Thompson. I recall that after the original conference I had to dash off to Washington, but I mention that in my account of activities in the USA.

Of course my visits to China also included opportunities to visit many of the chief tourist attractions including the Forbidden City, the Temple of Heaven and the Summer and Winter Palaces in Beijing; the Great Wall; the Ming Tombs; and the terra-cotta warriors in Xian. The trip to Xian was particularly interesting. During it I bought an egg-shell thin porcelain bowl as a memento which has pride of place in one of our rooms. One final memory is of attending with several colleagues an excellent Burns Night dinner at the British Embassy, at which the haggis was piped in by a piper who had been flown in earlier by BA.

South Africa (RSA)

I first went to RSA, not long after I had joined the Partnership, to respond to an invitation from Dr G J (Gerrie) Stander who was Chairman of that country's Water Research Commission. Gerrie was also Chairman of the International Association of Water Pollution Research (IAWPR) and I had had previous meetings with him at IAWPR conferences.

At about the same time B & P set up a local firm in RSA, entering into a collaborative relationship with a premier local consulting firm Ninham Shand and Partners, with a view to undertaking joint projects. Ninham Shand's Partner in Pretoria, where the Water Research Commission was based, was Jan de Wet, and I was very lucky to be able to work with Jan on numerous visits. My good fortune was magnified by the excellent hospitality that Jan and his delightful wife, Anne, afforded me throughout my visits, putting me up in their home, allowing me to take part in many of their recreational activities and taking me to stay in their holiday home in Hermanus, a coastal resort not very far from Cape Town (Plate 42). Jan was, indeed still is, a member of the Pretoria Country Club and took me on many delightful occasions to play golf there; and we also played during my visit to Hermanus. Jan and Anne have been very good friends throughout and we endeavour to return the hospitality they so generously gave us in RSA whenever they come to the UK.

Shortly after the local firm was set up, with offices in Johannesburg and Cape Town, we were appointed to advise the Water Research Commission (WRC) on appropriate means of treating the wastewaters from chrome and vegetable tanneries and fellmongeries. This involved visiting a series of these establishments to examine the current practice, initiation of several research projects to examine the performance of various treatment processes that were not at that time in use in the local industry and liaison with the Leather Industries Research Institute (LIRI) based in Grahamstown. Quite often I went with Alex Kinmont one of the WRC's senior executives. One of the projects was the subject of a paper by Mike Hagger, operating then from our local office, describing a new scheme for pre-treating tannery wastes by dissolved-air flotation prior to more conventional biological treatment.

Another project, again for the RSA Water Research Commission, required a major review of the then current technology for treatment and disposal of municipal sewage sludges and preparation of proposals for a study tour by a South African team in Germany, France and England. The project, which occupied several months at the end of 1978, went largely according to plan and as one might have expected generated a report, about $1^1/_2$ inches thick; this appeared to be well received by the client.

Another fascinating experience was a visit to Windhoek where the full-scale plant for recovering potable water from sewage effluent and recycling it into the town's domestic supply was operating. At the time the reclaimed water formed about 15% of the total domestic supply. The scheme worked satisfactorily for quite some years but I believe has now been superseded by the introduction of new supplies from conventional sources.

I was subsequently involved, though to a small extent, in a variety of projects, mainly generated by the enterprise of our local partner, Mr R C (Rodney) Squires who had moved into RSA from Hong Kong where he did notable work on various projects, especially the design of the HK Oceanarium. One of these involved visits to several abattoirs to initiate trials of a method of treating the wastewater, not previously used in RSA, by addition of sodium ligno-sulphonate to precipitate and recover protein. Though I much enjoy eating meat I always found rather unsettling in visits to abattoirs, the sight of rows of cattle or sheep, often plaintively mooing or bleating, or of chickens strung upside down from conveyor belts en route to the slaughter chambers in which the blood is collected via open channels for its recovery as a fertilizer. I couldn't help hoping however unrealistically that one day man will find a way of synthesizing appetising foodstuffs so as to preclude the need for slaughter other than perhaps for culling.

Around this time Colin Appleyard, an expert on industrial effluent treatment, as I mention elsewhere, joined the RSA firm to assist Rodney, and had a key role in several additional projects concerned with the control of pollution from local industries. One in particular, for the Water Research Commission, was a substantial study of Water and Effluent Management in the Fruit and Vegetable Industry.

A subsequent project was concerned with the prospect for treating water and wastewaters by a new process being researched in RSA known as cross-flow microfiltration. In essence the process involved filtration of particle bearing liquids through a porous tube through which the liquid was pumped at a sufficiently high velocity to scour off adherent deposits. My involvement was, however, conducted mainly in our London laboratory rather than in RSA as noted earlier.

I had two further memorable visits to RSA. One was in 1980, in my capacity as President of the Institute of Water Pollution Control. Every alternate year the President at the time visits RSA usually to attend the Annual Conference of the South African Branch of the Institute, and meetings with their local groups; and I was fortunate that my year involved such a visit on which Kathy accompanied me. I gave a Presidential Address in which I chose to concentrate on technical rather than political matters on the grounds that I had reviewed the latter in my address to Conference in London. I greatly enjoyed my meetings with the local groups some of which were in places I had not visited previously such as Durban, where I was able to have a round of golf, and Port Elizabeth. But undoubtedly one of the most rewarding experiences was spending three days at Skukuza in the Kruger National Park. We went with A R (Tony) Pitman and his then wife. Plate 40 shows the Pitmans and Kath at the venue. Kath and I agree that seeing a wide range of animals in their natural habitat in wonderfully tranquil surroundings was one of the most rewarding travel experiences we have ever had.

My last visit to RSA, towards the end of 1992, was triggered by the firm being appointed to advise the Municipal governing body of Istanbul on the design of a new treatment plant to serve a population of about $3\frac{1}{2}$ million to be located at Baltimani on the Bosphorus. The engineering department of the city council had apparently decided that because they thought it would not be long before Turkey joined the European Community the plant effluent should comply with the then latest EC standards for protection of sensitive water bodies requiring among other things that the contents of the algal nutrient nitrogen (N) and phosphorus (P) should not exceed quite stringent low limits. Personally I thought this was distinctly premature, in view of the absence so far as I was aware of quantification of the nutrient loads from other countries outside EC and their impacts, and the uncertainty both of the entry of Turkey to EC and the standards that would then be imposed. It would have been more prudent to assess the costs and benefits of possible options before making a choice. (However, if that was what the client was determined to have, so be it).

The Partner in charge of the project was David Kell (with whom as I mention elsewhere I had worked in Port Said and in preparing two papers for a conference in Istanbul) and he had co-opted in support my former colleague Arthur Boon who by this time had moved out of WRc into private practice. At a preliminary stage in the project I had made some rough estimates of the sort of facilities I thought would be needed using a rather 'steam-driven' method of manual calculation set out in one of a set of volumes on wastewater treatment, of which the principal editor was my old friend Wes Eckenfelder. (One of the volumes included a chapter I had contributed on European Practice.) My rudimentary effort was swiftly superseded by Arthur who had access to the latest computer models and put forward a novel design involving removal of the declining content of nitrogen in a 'plug-flow' reactor stage ultimately by endogenous respiration of the biomass. I imagined this method could well have guaranteed achievement of the desirable objective of good sludge settleability. By chance, at around this time, the IAWQ had arranged a study tour in RSA on 'Nutrient Removal and Anaerobic Digestion' and on behalf of the firm I went on the tour, accompanied by Kath.

The tour began in Johannesburg and we were soon made aware that the city was not as safe as I remembered it because a small party of Italian delegates was held up at knife-point and robbed within about 50 yards of the hotel in which we were staying (the Burgerspark). We moved on to visit a series of nutrient removal plants in the Transvaal area and then went on to see several more around Cape Town. We were kept well informed about the development of the plants, their design and performance by talks from many of the most notable pioneers in nutrient removal including Dr James Barnard, Mr A R (Tony) Pitman (with whom Kath and I had gone to the Kruger Park 12 years previously, as mentioned earlier), Dr C Viljoen (of the Rand Water Board), Prof G V R Marais and his successor Professor (George) Ekama at Cape Town University. I was particularly pleased to meet George Ekama for the first time because as it happened I had been an External Examiner for his PhD thesis. I had thought his thesis had been an excellent one not just because, as I told him jokingly, he had concluded inter alia that my theories on nitrification were correct. The last part of the tour concentrated on anaerobic treatment and membrane technology. The social side of the tour was a most pleasurable complement to the excellent technical presentations. We particularly enjoyed visits to wineries around Stellenbosch and in Kath's case, while I was otherwise engaged, a whale watching trip along the coast north of Cape Town.

In my report, with all its appendices over half an inch thick, I concluded that nothing I had seen caused me to question the technical feasibility of the process proposed for Baltimani though I see looking at the Report now I had some reservations about the sizing of the reactor stages. However I went on to add that the tour had confirmed my impression that an internal recycling system of the type I had seen operating successfully would be a viable option and (though I did not say so in the Report), could be regarded in effect as 'proven' technology, albeit on South African and not Istanbul sewage. My personal feeling was that since entry to E C was not imminent (indeed has still not taken place, twelve years on) the Turkish client would have been well advised to carry out pilot-scale trials of the proposed design. However my impression from the sidelines was that they probably would not have had the patience to do that. As it happened they were displaced from office a few months later and the project went into abeyance (and as far as I am aware this is still the situation).

Hong Kong

Our Hong Kong (HK) firm was the largest within the B & P group by a considerable margin and I made many visits there. After the first two or three visits I got used to what always seemed another 'hairy' landing at Kai Tak airport, in which it seemed one could almost shake hands with occupants of the upper floors in the buildings adjacent to the flight path. One always knew that one had reached one's destination however because the odour rising from Kai Tak nullah, a typhoon shelter into which a good deal of domestic wastes were

released, had a characteristic all of its own. All of this is now a thing of
the past, however, with the introduction of the new airport which I
have not had the opportunity to visit.

Most of my visits were of short duration involving minor inputs
into often quite large projects or job offers generated by other
Partners. In my first visit I gave a lecture, to a meeting of the HK
Engineering Society, that was subsequently published in the Society's
Journal dealing with 'Some Aspects of Research into Problems of
Water Pollution Control'. Somewhat presumptuously on that visit, I
had booked into the famous Peninsula Hotel and to my surprise just
ahead of me waiting to check in was a rather grumpy Danny Kaye.
What had upset him I never discovered but it made an intriguing start
to a much enjoyed albeit short stay in the hotel. My visits afforded me
many pleasant social or recreational experiences including rounds of
golf at Fanling, visits to Macau and Lantau, the Rugby Sevens annual
tournament, horse-racing at Happy Valley, getting suits and shirts
tailor-made often in less than two days at prices well below those in
UK, and on one occasion watching from the Yacht Club the fireworks
display in the Harbour during the Chinese New Year by courtesy of
our senior local partner, Mr A J (Tony) Vail, OBE. It was either on that
or another occasion that Kath and I stayed with Tony and his wife at
their home not far from Fanling in the New Territories and then went
on to take part in a project at Fresno, California, that I mention
elsewhere. On another visit I arrived on the day of the Consulting
Engineers' Annual Dinner, a black tie event, and was immediately
invited to attend. I didn't have a dinner jacket with me and there
wasn't time to hire one. However I did have a dark blue suit and a
white shirt so I borrowed a bow tie and went in the resulting
ensemble. After the dinner at which the Governor was the principal
guest he came round to shake hands and chat with other members and
guests. When he reached me I said, 'I'm sorry to be here improperly
dressed, Governor,' to which he replied, 'Oh don't worry, you've
really got quite a good disguise.'

In the early eighties I took part in a project led by Stanley Ford, one of our most notable London partners, who was also a Senior Partner of the Hong Kong firm. The project was to provide a preliminary appraisal of the likely effects of the discharge of effluent from the burgeoning new towns of Sha Tin and Tai Po on the waters of Tolo Harbour and of treatment processes that might be required at these cities to prevent adverse impact on the Harbour waters. Inevitably in the absence of a water quality model such appraisals had to be approximate and subjective. We had collaboration in these appraisals with an American firm (TOUPS are the initials that stick in my mind) and a particularly enjoyable consequence was that their engineer in HK arranged for me to make a tour of several of the most advanced treatment facilities in California.

I was accompanied by Dr Frank Wood, a chemical engineer who had been 'recruited' from the Atomic Energy Authority to assist Stanley Ford and Jack Gardiner in the design of a new desalination plant for the colony at Lok on Pai (Plate 22). At the time the stimulus for introduction of the plant, the first major multi-stage flash plant in the world, was uncertainty about the continued availability of supplies of fresh water from the Chinese mainland. However apart from the initial successful proving trials the plant has been largely 'mothballed' as the worries about the mainland supply were eventually put aside.

Included among the treatment facilities Frank Wood and I visited in California was the particularly impressive Water Factory 21 in which sewage effluent from a conventional plant was given further treatment to produce water of potable quality. However instead of being used directly for that purpose (unlike the practice at Windhoek in South Africa) the water was injected into the ground to form a barrier preventing intrusion of salt water from the nearby coast into the ground water drawn on for potable supply.

My largest involvement in HK was as the technical leader in a subsequent project to develop for the HK Environmental Protection

Department (EPD) mathematical models for forecasting the effects of polluting discharges, from Sha Tin and Tai Po, on water quality and ecology in the estuarine regime of Tolo Harbour in the New Territories; and also for indicating means of preventing the increasing occurrence of so-called 'red tides' caused by proliferation of toxic red algae or dinoflagellates. The project was technically very interesting because the estuary water was stratified both vertically and horizontally, thus requiring development of a 3-D model. Up to that time I believe there had been few if any 3-D water quality models, and certainly no ecosystem models for this type of estuarial system. Plate 39 shows a view of one part of the Harbour and Plate 41 an inner area, as seen by looking down from a vantage point in Sha Tin (above the new racecourse).

In view of my earlier contacts with the Hydraulics Research Laboratory and the Institution of Marine Environmental Research, especially in connection with Severn Tidal Power, I was fortunately able to enlist them on repayment terms to provide the major inputs needed to produce the requisite model.

The time and finance allocated to the project and the available historical water quality data were, unsurprisingly, insufficient to provide models embodying all the detailed features ideally required or to do more than minimal validation of the models' predictions. Nevertheless the model suite furnished was we felt a good basic framework on which the EPD could build.

We were also required to give training in the development and use of the models to EPD staff. I recall that in our final meeting with EPD they at first expressed disappointment with the extent of training we were able to give but after we had explained the difficulties in bringing staff not originally versed in the complex technology 'up-to-speed' in quite a short time they accepted the position.

During my penultimate visit to Hong Kong, as one of the invited speakers, I gave a paper on 'Strategic Planning of Water Quality' in an international conference on Pollution in the Environment, POLMET

85. Also among those giving papers were my old friend Geoff Truesdale, Rodney Squires, Ray Groves, Russell Bowler and Roy Oakley (of Watson Hawksley). Rodney and Ray talked about the scope for the cross-flow microfiltration process I refer to elsewhere.

Three years later I again gave an invited paper to POLMET 88, this time with as my co-authors A R R (Arthur) Lupton (our firm's mathematical expert) and Alvin Smith. Our subject was the 'Use of Models in Control of Water Quality'. Though I have no recollection of presenting the paper I do recall being a little disappointed at the time because in the paper we postulated that there might be circumstances in which nitrification of ammonia might be prevented in estuaries by the hydraulic 'wash-out' of nitrifying bacteria. This was a challenging hypothesis running counter to the usual assumption and one on which I would have welcomed some 'feedback' from participants – but none was forthcoming. Again there were quite a few old friends at the conference including Dr Stuart Reed and Paul Holmes of the HK EPD, Professor Roger Perry (Imperial College, London), Tony Vail the Senior Partner of our HK firm, and David Thom from New Zealand.

Kath and I subsequently went with Paul Holmes and his wife Brenda to a conference in Holland, just around the time that he returned to work again in the UK, and we exchange cards regularly at Christmas. My only other (typically rather vague) recollection is of taking part in a discussion session concerned with the means of providing water supplies and pollution control facilities in developing countries. I think I again generated some controversy by contending that what was wanted was not so much new methods but generation of the necessary finance to apply existing technology.

My final visit must have been in 1994 when I presented a paper on 'Treatment of Water and Wastewater' to what was called 'The World Congress on Urban Growth and the Environment'. As far as I know the papers given were not originally published. However early in the following year I received an invitation, which I accepted, to have a

shortened version (1500-2000 words) published in the journal Water
& Wastewater International.

USA

After I joined B & P I made several more visits to the States. The first
one was at the end of 1974 when, following an invitation from Wes
Eckenfelder, I gave a paper at an International Conference (sponsored
by IAWPR) in New Orleans on 'Effluent Variability from Wastewater
Treatment Processes and its Control'. My paper concentrated, of
course, on UK experience. I recall little of the conference other than
that many old friends were among the authors; and still less of New
Orleans apart from the 'coffins on stilts'. However as it happens I still
have a volume of the Proceedings.

In my Presidential year (1979-80) I went together with Kath to the
US Water Pollution Control Federation's Annual Conference at
Houston. This was an interesting and enjoyable event at which I again
met many old friends and made some new ones. One of the latter was
Dr Takeshi Kubo of the Research Institute of Wastewater Management
in Tokyo, who in his distinguished career did a great deal to enhance
the status of pollution control in Japan, to foster very fruitful
exchanges of ideas, information and training facilities especially with
the USA and in the late nineties was the well-deserving recipient of
the Stockholm Water Prize. Plate 43 shows Takeshi with me in one of
the offices in B & P's HQ in Redhill when he came to talk to me
about UK pollution control practices. Takeshi and his wife Masako
have met with Kath and me in London and we exchange messages and
greetings regularly, especially at Christmas. Kath greatly enjoyed
herself on a visit to NASA Space Station in Houston. To my regret I
couldn't accompany her as there was some business to attend to on
that day.

My next visit, in 1981, was to present a paper on 'Modelling the
Effects of Pollution on Estuaries' to a conference convened by the
American Society of Chemical Engineers in New York. Typically

almost all I remember is staying in a hotel (I think a Sheraton) just round the corner from Central Park; and being advised not to go into the Park after dark for fear of being mugged.

On one return journey from the States to the UK in 1983 I gave a paper that George Eden and I had prepared to a USEPA Workshop at Clemson University, South Carolina, on 'Low-Cost Wastewater Treatment'. Our paper was entitled 'Disposal of Sewage in Coastal Waters – the British Experience'. Actually our paper centred on disposal of sewage to sea through pipelines after only preliminary treatment by screening and we justified its inclusion not because this method was intrinsically cheap but because it was much less expensive than providing full-treatment on land before release close to the shore. I recall that this didn't seem to go down too well with some of the representatives of the USEPA, I think from their research laboratory in Cincinnati, who perhaps because of their inland location appeared to consider this an undesirable practice.

One other interesting facet was afforded by a paper advocating the use of fill-and-draw plants (in the style of the one I refer to in Plate 7). This coincided with an up-surge of interest in such plants, generated by among others, an old friend from Australia, Merv Goronszy.

Most of my last few visits to the USA arose initially from some 'prospecting' conducted by Rodney Squires, with his customary entrepreneurial skill, in which he had discovered that a problem had arisen in California owing to the presence of selenium in drainage water from the fruit growing areas in the San Joaquin Valley not far from Fresno. The drainage water had been conveyed to a small impounding lake with a view to conveying it subsequently to San Francisco Bay. However, it soon became evident that birds populating the lake were producing deformed chicks as a consequence of the presence of the selenium in the water. The selenium, which was a natural component of the subsoil in the area drained, attained concentrations in the drainage water of around 350 micrograms per litre (μg/l). Rodney referred the problem to us in London and we undertook experiments in our Hide Place Laboratory to find a method of removing the selenium. It seemed obvious that this could be done by reverse-osmosis but that seemed likely to be much too expensive. After exploring various other possibilities we finally found a biochemical process sequence, which we thought might 'fit the bill'. This consisted of passing the water through an anoxic reactor, 'fuelled' by methanol, to remove nitrate, and then through an anaerobic reactor in which the selenium (initially present as selenate ion) was reduced and absorbed. Residual particles were removed by cross-flow microfiltration. As a precaution, or perhaps with misguided optimism, we patented the process. By this time Rodney had decided to move to the States and he set up a local firm, EPOC Inc, in Fresno and formed associations with a Californian firm, whose leader was Webb Cullington.

Rodney secured a contract with the State of California Department of Water Resources to test out the process more thoroughly and arranged the installation of a pilot-plant in Murrieta Farm near Fresno. This plant was supervised by B & P's geotechnical expert Dr A N (Tony) James and run with the help of a small team that had mostly been on Rodney's staff in RSA. The object was to establish the conditions required to reduce the selenium content of the drainage water from around 350 μg/l to about 10 μg/l or lower, the standard that had been set by the USEPA. The plant proved capable of reducing selenium nearly to the required standard but, even if that might have sufficed, the local farming community considered the likely costs unacceptably high. In an attempt to reduce costs the team examined the possibility of replacing the relatively expensive methanol with a sugar mill waste. This proved only moderately effective. However, at this point the whole matter became the subject of legal wrangles from which as far as B & P were concerned it never emerged.

Another facet of these studies, supervised by Tony James, was that the farm drainage water also contained in addition to selenium concentrations of boron (probably as borate ion) often in excess of

10 μg/l. It seemed possible that the borate was restricting formation of both the anoxic and anaerobic conditions necessary for selenium removal. Thus the opportunity was taken to examine the extent of removal of boron attainable by passing filtered effluent from the pilot-plant through a column of a commercially available boron-specific ion-exchange resin. This reduced the boron content of the pilot-plant effluent to less than 1 μg/l and also reduced the residual content of selenium slightly.

On one occasion during the project Kath and I went on from Hong Kong to Fresno to enable me to discuss progress with Rodney, Tony and Webb Cullington. We had a great time staying at a motel in Fresno. Either the Motel didn't serve breakfast or it was more expedient to get the meal at a restaurant across the road but the latter is what we did. We were quite intrigued when each morning just before eight o'clock the breakfast room was invaded by a cavalcade of local farmers or farm hands who demolished the food in next to no time then just as suddenly disappeared with much jostling and sounding of car horns. We were also able to play a couple of rounds of golf on the local courses and then on what we were told was the President's Birthday weekend we had an excellent trip to Monterey, well briefed by the legal adviser to our US Associates and his wife, a most hospitable couple, who lent us two sets of golf clubs to take with us. The trip to Monterey afforded the opportunity to watch the seals and sea lions on the rocks in the Bay, briefly to see Cannery Row, to take the renowned 17-mile drive round the area, and visit Clint Eastwood's mayoral town of Carmel. We had thought of playing Pebble Beach golf course but when I learned that this would cost us $180 I'm afraid I baulked at the idea (though of course that sort of sum would not now be unusual on many European courses). Instead we went to Carmel but the course there was so crowded that we had to be content with hitting balls on the driving range.

On one of my visits to California I was flying in from somewhere well to the west. On this occasion, because of complexities with connecting flights, our travel girl in the London office arranged for me to have a stopover in Honolulu and what's more, since we were then normally travelling by Business Class, a flight in 1st Class from there to San Francisco. I had an enjoyable evening in a hotel near the famous Waikiki Beach of which I managed to get a quick glimpse the following morning. I remember the subsequent flight of about 4 hours' duration if only because I had the pleasure of lounging back after a splendid lunch watching one of the few (perhaps the only) films that Pavarotti has made (a treacly romance but without much singing).

My last visit came at the end of a particularly busy stint in China when I then had to dash off to Washington to attend the IAWPR's biennial conference; and more particularly to lecture in a study course that Wes Eckenfelder had once again organized to accompany the conference. I was by this time somewhat drained and under-prepared for the study course. As a result I spent a good deal of time when I would have preferred to be at the conference in my hotel room getting the material for my lectures ready. Of particular regret in that regard was having to miss the visit of delegates to the Smithsonian Institute. But I managed to discharge my obligations adequately I think and certainly enjoyed a final dinner with some of the many old friends that I encountered during the visit.

Malaysia

I made numerous visits to Malaysia, mainly to provide short inputs to projects being carried out originally by our local firm and later by its successor. In the original firm the Senior Partner was a Partner from the UK firm and the others were Malaysians or in one case Chinese. Two of the latter that I got to know best were Hooi Kahung, who is Chinese in ethnic origin, and Syed (now Dato Syed) Mohammed Shahabuddin. After some years the firm evolved into a Bumiputra organization of which Syed became the senior executive. My first involvement was near the end of 1974 when I gave a paper on

'Advances in the Treatment of Sewage and Industrial Wastewaters with Specific Reference to the Reclamation of Water for Re-use', to the Malaysian Institution of Engineers. Projects I was subsequently involved in though very marginally included studies of the impacts on water quality in rivers in the Muar basin, Klang Valley, Sungai Linggi basin, the South Coastal Trengganu region and in the Kuantan area. The last two projects took me for the first time to the east coast which had some very attractive features. In the course of such studies I inevitably visited a number of rubber and palm oil production units many of which had quite effective effluent treatment facilities and which incidentally I was able to feature in my lectures in Delft. Plate 52 shows part of the treatment plant at one palm-oil mill.

It was following my visit to Kuantan and other towns on the east coast around 1980 that on the evening that I returned to my hotel in Kuala Lumpur I began to experience chest pains that continued through the night and I thought at first were due to indigestion. However they persisted and the following morning I went to see the local firm's doctor. He told me he thought I'd got a heart problem and I'd better go to the main general hospital in KL. One of the firm's younger environmental engineers (I think with Spanish forebears) took me in his car and when we reached the hospital he said, 'Wait a moment until I've had a look inside.' When he came out he said, 'I don't think you'd better go in there, the culture shock might finish you off', (though remember this was nearly twenty-five years ago). So he took me off to a private clinic where they looked after me very well, to the extent that I had recovered from the ischaemic episode, as they described it, within about two days. Meanwhile my thoughtful partners in the UK had kindly arranged for Kath to fly out to give me support. There was some delay because she had to break the journey with an overnight stop in Bangkok, and she was astonished when arriving at KL airport to find that I was waiting there to meet her. I had been advised to take things easy for a few days, so we spent them very agreeably by relaxing in a holiday hotel in Penang.

52. Wastewater treatment plant at a palm-oil mill in Malaysia.

In my last visit in the early nineties I was engaged to advise on national water quality standards that were being prepared to protect the country's rivers. I recall liaising with a Malaysian Chinese professor who was similarly engaged and having quite a few friendly arguments with him about the proposed limits for several quality characteristics. I suppose having a somewhat pragmatic UK approach and thinking of Malaysia as more of a developing than a developed country, I advocated rather more relaxed standards than some of those laid down in the European Community. Uppermost in my mind was the desirability of not saddling the country with excessive financial burdens. My 'co-worker', probably better informed than me about the pace of development, wanted significantly tighter standards. I think in the event at least some of his recommendations were accepted by the Government and with hindsight the rapid growth in the Malaysian economy made me think that I had been unduly pessimistic about what would be affordable.

I have particularly happy memories of the time spent socially with Syed and his wife, Akman, in the UK and KL. I last saw them in 2002 when they were entertaining at a London hotel a number of those in the firm with whom they had had the closest contacts. I was delighted to receive from Syed a pewter letter holder of which the front is a replica of the KL skyline around the Sultan Abdul Samad Building. I also well remember some good golf games that Richard Phillips, Nick Dawes and I had with Syed.

I delivered papers and addresses at a number of local conferences. At one of these, PROCHEM ASIA'84 organized by the Instituit KIMIA Malaysia, I was scheduled to give the opening address on 'Advances in Effluent Treatment Technology', but as I mention in the section on China my journey from Guangzhou was delayed. I had alerted Nick Dawes, who at the time was the firm's senior resident Partner in KL, that I might be late and he kindly agreed to stand in for me if, as he put it, 'the worst came to the worst'. Fortunately I arrived just in time and a very nice framed metal plate with which I was presented by the organisers has been hanging in my office ever since. On my last visit I gave a talk at a symposium on 'Water Resources Development Projects' and Plate 53 shows Syed presenting me with a gift of appreciation.

Indonesia

In all of the several visits I made to Indonesia I was based in Jakarta where our firm had local offices. In my only visit outside Jakarta I went inland to Bandung, among other things to meet with a Professor there who had attended one of the courses of lectures that I gave each year at Delft. Most of my involvements were minor contributions to projects on various aspects of pollution control.

My single most important project, albeit still a small one, was to produce an embryonic water quality model for the Kali Sunter, one of Jakarta's major rivers on the east side of the city and a grossly polluted one (Plate 46). I describe the model as embryonic because although I

53. Being presented with a 'gift of appreciation' in Kuala Lumpur.

obtained a reasonably plausible reconciliation between the observed distribution of dissolved oxygen and that predicted using the model this was for only a narrow range of conditions to which the very limited observations available related.

I enjoyed all my visits, becoming quite fond of Indonesian food especially Nasi Goreng. I did, however, get many more mosquito bites than I cared for despite the use of various prophylactics. One final misfortune arose when on the night before an early morning flight to Hong Kong I put out the remaining clean clothes that I had on top of a large shelf in my hotel room. On the following morning I awoke to find that the clothes were all soaked owing to a failure in the air conditioning system beneath which I had without noticing positioned them. I arrived back in Hong Kong in a somewhat scruffy condition.

New Zealand

My first visit to New Zealand, the result of some prospecting by one of our Chief Engineers, Joe Stewart, was to examine pollution from an outfall at Napier Hastings on the west coast of the North Island, and to advise on remedial measures. En route I stayed in a motel on the outskirts of Auckland and just before breakfast there was a sudden thump and the building seemed to shiver slightly. Immediately I thought someone had driven their car into the building. It was not until I went into breakfast that I was made aware that it was an earth tremor, something I had never before experienced. This gave me a slight sense of foreboding as Napier where I was headed had been the site of a serious earthquake some years previously – though on that score I need not have worried because nothing further of that kind occurred. In a sense I became slightly more alarmed by my experience when I proceeded on by a very small light plane (virtually a two-seater) which had been arranged to give me an aerial view of the outfall and neighbouring coast. The young pilot said, 'I hope you won't mind if on the way I practise a few of my tight turns.' This quite worried me when they happened because I had a simple strap safety belt and was sitting next to a door with just a simple lever opener handle – indeed it reminded me very much of the arrangement in my first car, the 1936 BSA Scout mentioned earlier. When the pilot banked and turned I found myself looking it seemed straight down at the sea with the feeling that 'two clicks and I'll be down in the drink'. Of course nothing like that happened and I had an excellent view of the site. This was fascinating because parts of the sea for about 200m (220 yards) around the outfall was coloured literally blood red because the water discharged contained a large component from local abattoirs (Plate 44). I cannot remember what I recommended precisely but I imagine that it was for introduction of some pre-treatment of the abattoir wastes and more definitely that a new pipeline be laid to discharge the wastes about 1km offshore. I believe that something of this kind was done and so far as I know the scheme has proved satisfactory.

After my visit to the site the local chief engineer (whose name regretfully eludes me) kindly took me on a circular tour embracing the more southerly parts of the Island and including Lake Taupo. Plate 50 shows him at one of our stops en route. This tour turned out to have more technical relevance than I had supposed because around this time my Partner, Tom Hammond, had obtained an appointment for the firm to develop a scheme to supplement Auckland's water supply using as a source the Waikato River the headwaters of which originated in the Lake. Two of the firm's younger engineers had set up a very neat pilot plant to undertake treatability studies and I remember thinking when I saw it that it would stand comparison with many that we had at WPRL and more relevantly perhaps those at WRA. One of the engineers was John Davies with whom I had occasional working involvements subsequently including one in Ukraine (see later). Our firm had formed as association with a local firm, Kingston, Reynolds, Thom and Allardyce, and I have many happy memories of subsequent meetings with their Partner, David Thom, both in New Zealand, London and also on one occasion in Hong Kong. Of the bizarre things that somehow stick in one's memory I recall David Thom, knowing of my easily punctured skin, warning me that in Auckland the 'mosquitoes were as big as helicopters'. Other memories of Auckland are of enjoyable stays in a hotel called I think the South Pacific which had a huge marlin in a case hanging over the fireplace in the reception area; and being told that a temporary steel extension, built by the Japanese, to one of the harbour bridges was known locally as the 'Nippon Clip on'.

Reverting briefly to my tour in the North Island, on the last lap of the trip we visited the Wairacki geothermal power station. There we found an open-air swimming pool heated by the geothermal spring and as by this time we were at the end of the 'working' day we went in for a swim. It was quite dark and the general ambience was rather akin to that in the UK on a foggy November night. However I can't remember anything more relaxing than bathing in the warm water as we did that night.

In a later visit to give a lecture at Palmerston North in a conference that the indefatigable Wes Eckenfelder had helped to organize I came in on a flight via Australia on the previous limb of which my luggage had gone astray. The airline (Qantas) said, 'Well we expect to find your luggage swiftly but meanwhile when you get to Auckland call in at the terminal building and collect the $25 to which you are entitled to get whatever you need to tide you over.' In those days Auckland was really quite a small airport and when I went to collect my cash the local staff said, 'Wait a moment while we get the cash box.' As it happened an old acquaintance in the water industry (Ron Hicks) had come over to say 'Howdo' prior to my departure on a connecting flight to Palmerston North, which we could see warming up on the tarmac. When the staff brought the cash box it looked not unlike a child's moneybox but they couldn't get it open. Seeing that my flight's departure was imminent my friend said, 'Well you go on and I'll mail you the money when they get it open.' The following day he rang me and said, 'You're not going to believe this but after about half an hour they finally got the box open and, guess what, there was only $8 in there!'

After my lecture in the Course I was taken for afternoon tea by the wife of one of the organizers and seated in front of a blazing log fire. By this time being tired and heavily jet lagged and pleasantly warm I did what I have never done before or since, I fell asleep while my hostess was talking to me. That gaffe apart I thoroughly enjoyed my time in New Zealand, including subsequent very minor involvements in other projects, and envy some of my local friends in Stevenage PROBUS Club (see later) who go off at intervals to visit relatives there.

Ukraine

One of my last overseas assignments for the firm involved a short but very interesting visit to Ukraine in the mid-nineties as a member of a team assembled by the lead firm Coopers and Lybrand (C & L). One of the team members was John Davies with whom I had worked in New Zealand, when at that time he was with our firm. The objective was to identify projects that might be suitable for financing from the European Development Fund, and my role was to comment on the status of water and wastewater treatment facilities in that context. I flew from London to Kiev and from there took an overnight train to Zaporodze, a major city on the banks of the River Dnepr (UK spelling Dnieper) about 200 miles (320 km) from the Black Sea. As it happened a few days before leaving for Kiev I went by train from Stevenage to Newcastle (to act if I remember correctly as external examiner for a PhD student from the Public Health Engineering Department of the University). The distance of the journey, about 270 miles (430km) was by coincidence about the same as that from Kiev to Zaporodze but whereas the UK journey took about $2^{1}/_{2}$ hours, that in Ukraine took about 15 hours travelling overnight. I shared a 4-berth sleeping compartment with two Ukrainian businessmen who apparently spoke not a word of English and since the only Russian words I knew were *niet, da* and *groos vendenji'* (I can pronounce it but can't be sure of the spelling) communication was limited to sign language. Another problem was that the station names appeared in Cyrillic script and so were incomprehensible to me. Interestingly the station platforms were much lower than ours being so far as I could judge only about two feet above the ground. As our ETA approached I began to wonder whether I would know when to get out, especially since I think someone had told me that Zaporodze had three stations. However, fortunately Coopers and Lybrand had briefed the train staff to get me off at the right place and when the train halted a burly Ukrainian lady from among their number suddenly appeared uttering, 'Out', and leaving me in no doubt that I had reached my destination. The first thing that struck me on doing so was the chill in the air (it was late February or early March); in fact the temperatures at midday during my five days in Zaporodze were usually around 15°C below zero.

The hotel I was taken to was pleasantly warm inside though I had water warm enough to shower in on only one day out of the five. Most of the other members of the team were also staying in the hotel and we had some pleasant dinners together after the day's work was done. These meals were always accompanied much to my pleasure by Asti Spumante, which appeared to be the only recognizable wine available.

My time was taken up by visits to the water treatment and sewage treatment plants, drainage facilities, a range of industrial establishments and a large lagoon into which industrial wastewaters were released.

The water treatment plant drew its supply from the Dnepr and an intriguing aspect of conversation arose because Zaporodze is not very far from Chernobyl and when the explosion in the nuclear reactor occurred (a year or two before our visit) the fall-out of fission products contaminated the river. I was told that, as soon as possible after the explosion, to protect domestic consumers the works' management had ingeniously replaced some of the sand in the works' sand filters by ground Clinotilolite, a naturally occurring cation-exchange mineral, which could certainly have been expected to remove radiostrontium, probably the most dangerous component of the contamination. Broadly I considered that the water treatment plant was serving its purpose adequately, though several features of the facilities were two or three decades behind those of the most modern works in the UK and the USA.

My opinion of the sewage treatment works was very similar. I was quite intrigued when reaching the works to find it shrouded in a steam-like mist. The explanation was simply that the mist was the result of the interaction between cold outside air and the relatively warm sewage whose temperature was inflated by the presence of industrial cooling waters. In the UK release of cooling waters to the sewers is not usually permitted because they are normally relatively uncontaminated and would take up capacity unnecessarily in the drainage system. Apparently such restrictions were not operative in Zaporodze. However, although sewer capacity was lost by this, a partial compensation was derived from the fact that the higher temperature of the sewage enabled nitified effluents to be produced in winter in somewhat shorter residence-times and thus smaller plants than is possible in the UK.

In regard to industrial wastewaters there were considerable imperfections in the legislative controls relative to those prevailing in the UK and other EC countries both for releases to river and to sewers. However the Government was pursuing a policy of gradually improving environmental protection, involving an annual review and if necessary revision of effluent standards. We understood that at the time we were there about 40% of the industries discharged effluent directly to the River Dnepr without treatment.

Because of constraints on time we were able to visit only one industry, a massive steel works, Zaporozhstal. There we observed that a number of conventional techniques were being used to foster re-circulation of suitable waste streams and to reduce the degree of contamination of others. The final mixture of nevertheless still quite contaminated wastewater was released to a large lagoon, which also received effluent from 7 other industries. We visited the lagoon which had a detention period of several weeks and as far as we could tell from visual inspection of the final discharge to the Dnepr, it had served to reduce the polluting load to river considerably, presumably mainly by sedimentation and biological breakdown of impurities. A fortunate feature was that the discharge from the lagoon entered the river downstream of the water supply intakes. However the long-term implications of the discharge on water quality in the river were a matter of speculation.

On the return overnight train journey to Kiev the whole team travelled together. This proved fortunate since locals who appeared to have consumed too much vodka paraded somewhat noisily up and down the corridors until the early hours. Back in Kiev we foregathered at (I think) the Intercontinental Hotel (not that far from the football stadium where Dynamo Kiev play) before returning to the UK.

Considering the overall objective of identifying facilities appropriate for EC funding, although the few we saw appeared to be performing adequately, we understood there were many massive deficiencies in for example the facts that the water treatment capacity was too small to meet demand, losses in the distribution system were unacceptably high, the sewage treatment capacity and that for industrial effluent treatment needed to be considerably increased. Although I was not involved in preparation of the final recommendations I saw a copy of the C & L report indicating that such matters were identified as among those having the highest priority for funding.

India

In addition to my two previous visits mentioned earlier I went briefly to India in the early eighties to assist Richard Phillips who supervised the firm's activities there in a job offer for the design of effluent treatment facilities for (if memory serves) a steel mill. I stayed in the world famous Taj Hotel in Bombay where I was very impressed with everything except perhaps the slight curry-like smell that pervaded many of the corridors. During this visit I attended a cocktail party hosted by Richard at which our main guests were members of Tata Engineering, the most important and largest engineering firm in India. I was chatting with Tata's Managing Director and somehow the conversation turned to golf (it would, wouldn't it). When he learned that I played he said, 'Right I'll fix you up with some clubs and we'll have 9 holes before work tomorrow at my Club (I think, the Wellesley). I'll send a car to collect you at 6.30 am!' The following morning somewhat bleary eyed (in my case) we set off from the first tee and I noticed that he was playing with a rather tatty looking white ball. To my surprise when we reached the green he replaced this ball before putting with a new-looking red one. Throughout our round he repeated this tactic, which I think may be against the rules, though I've never checked. However I thoroughly enjoyed the occasion and would have done so even if in addition I hadn't finished one-up.

Pakistan

Other than my experiences in Lahore on the rural water supply project mentioned earlier my other memories of Pakistan centre mainly on Lyallpur (now renamed Faisalabad) and Karachi. I made a small input into a project to upgrade the water and wastewater treatment facilities in Lyallpur. Fortunately I arrived there a few months after the start of the work by which time my colleagues had managed to convert the originally rather primitive quarters made available to them into reasonably habitable accommodation. Eating local foodstuffs was initially somewhat hazardous I gathered but fortunately the practice had evolved of dining in the house occupied by the team leader, Bob Darling, whose wife, Ruth, who had accompanied him supervised the preparation of the food including, when appropriate, dousing vegetables and salad ingredients in potassium permanganate. I'll have to confess to a mild sense of relief when my input was concluded.

On another occasion I was returning home from Lahore on a flight to Karachi scheduled to take off at around 6 p.m. We had no sooner boarded the aircraft than the Captain came through on the intercom to tell us that it was raining heavily in Karachi, that runways were flooded and to attempt to land would be too dangerous. We were taken back to the departure lounge but after a wait of an hour or so the weather had apparently improved so we went back on board. Unfortunately by this time the Karachi weather had again deteriorated so back we went again to the terminal. I think we finally got off about 5 hours late and arrived in Karachi in the early hours of the morning. It was still raining there but evidently not nearly as heavily as before and there was a long queue waiting for taxis. I was nearly at the back of the queue but suddenly a voice said, 'Psst, you want a cab Mister?'

Having nodded I was taken by a rather scruffy looking individual in a quick dash through the rain to a dilapidated vehicle in which we then set off back to my hotel. It wasn't until we got under way that I realized that the cab didn't have any windscreen wipers and to maintain visibility the driver had from time to time to open his door window, lean forward and with some sort of brush clear away the raindrops. Since the road from the airport to the city was badly littered with potholes I was mightily relieved to get back to the hotel in one piece.

By the time I got into bed it must have been about three o'clock in the morning but in what seemed like no time the phone rang, I think at about 7.30 a.m., and the cheery voice of the firm's local representative said, 'You'll be pleased to know that I've arranged for you to meet a potential client at 9 a.m!' I should like to be able to report that we got an assignment as a result, but we didn't.

Mauritius

In the late eighties or early nineties our South African firm started to look at the prospects for gaining work in Mauritius in collaboration with a local firm there. I was asked to call in there to do a bit of 'publicizing' on my way to another assignment in Indonesia. I duly did so, and because it seemed too good an opportunity to miss, Kath (plus golf clubs) came with me. We stayed at the excellent St Gerain Hotel which in addition to all its other attractions includes as readers might now expect a 9-hole golf course, some of the holes of which border the beach. Our associates had arranged for me to give a talk at a local conference preceded by an interview which I understood might be broadcast. I gave the interview but I doubt whether it was ever used, possibly at least in part because I found it difficult to get on the same wavelength as the interviewer who naturally enough was much more interested in the island's public water supply than pollution control. My talk at the conference seemed to be quite well received but regretfully I don't think our RSA firm got any significant work as a result. On the social side we thoroughly enjoyed our time in the hotel especially with mynah birds flying around the dining room at breakfast and lunch, excellent buffet dinners on the beach in the warm tropical darkness, snorkelling (in Kath's case) and touring round the island including the well-known resort at Tousseroq, plus Port Louis, Curepipe and mountainous volcanic areas. I was intrigued when playing the hotel golf course to find that when the ball landed on the fairway it did so with a dull thud and practically no forward roll even when hit without backspin. This I soon realized was essentially due to the very sandy nature of the subsoil, but this certainly didn't spoil our enjoyment. By coincidence the middle of our stay encompassed my birthday (on 27th March) and our wedding anniversary (on the 29th). Whether the hotel became aware of the former by looking at my passport I know not but certainly at dinner that night the band struck up with 'Happy Birthday'. Possibly I may at this point have mentioned our forthcoming anniversary to one of the hotel staff because on the evening of the 29th two glamorous young ladies came to take us to dinner; at least it would have been us but for the fact that little known to the hotel Kath had returned to the UK on that late afternoon's flight, whereas I was going off in the opposite direction to Indonesia the following morning. I think I still received musical congratulations from the band and I hope that, by this time, my appreciable suntan at least partially hid my embarrassment.

Portugal

Although I have been on golfing holidays to Portugal probably at least thirty times and I went on business for WPRL in the early sixties (as I mention earlier), my professional visits in subsequent private practice have been just two. The first was to prepare an offer of services for the treatment and disposal of wastewaters from the Algarve. This involved a tour with a colleague to most of the coastal towns in the Algarve prior to preparing an offer. I did not think we had much of a chance of success because another well known UK firm was competing for the project, already had work in Portugal and had been 'preparing the ground' well before our arrival; and so it proved.

My other involvement stemmed from an informal meeting I had in 1984 in Hamburg with Professor G Kullenburg and one or two others to discuss the venue for a proposed NATO Advanced Research Workshop on the 'Role of the Oceans as a Waste Disposal Option'. Someone, and it may well have been I, half jokingly said, 'How about the Algarve?' Well as it turned out when the matter was referred to the organizing committee, much to my satisfaction, Vilamoura, where I often went to play golf, was chosen as the location. As it happened my former fellow pupil at Arnold School, Martin Holdgate (mentioned earlier), who had joined the DoE several years previously, was a member of the organizing committee. The conference duly took place in April 1985 and taking advantage of the opportunity to combine business with pleasure I took Kath and Gill with me. I gave a paper entitled 'Sewage Treatment and Disposal – Constraints and Opportunities' which, among other things, included a review of the arguments for disposal of sewage from coastal towns to sea through submarine outfalls rather than treatment to high standards before release much nearer the shore. I illustrated this with brief accounts of two of the firm's projects, one at Ingoldmells on the UK's east coast and the other at Cape Peron near Perth, Western Australia. The Cape Peron scheme was of particular interest to me in view of the substantial time I had spent in Perth on other projects and I give a few more details of this in my account of my activities in Australia. I recall some lively interactions with some American delegates, who gave me the impression that they thought disposal of sewage to sea after no more than preliminary screening was a bit primitive, but our 'debates' did not figure in the official proceedings. After the conference was over, we had a most enjoyable golfing holiday – but that's another story.

Thailand

Apart from a couple of very short prospecting trips from Hong Kong with one of the local Partners there I had only a week or so's active work in Thailand. This was on a project led by Jeremy Goad with whom I had previously worked for short periods in London and Saudi Arabia, though in the latter case only by virtue of being Partner-in-Charge of a waste treatment project there (see later), when Jeremy was our local representative. The Bangkok project was a very interesting one because it involved developing design proposals for sewage treatment plants, for which the land area available was exceptionally small. I proposed, among other things, use of a then relatively new technique of aerated filtration for the main biological oxidation stage since the filters would have occupied a much smaller area than a conventional AS plant. Regretfully, yet again, I have lost touch with subsequent developments so I don't know what if anything has been built. During the project, which involved associated work in the UK, I was often in touch with Frank Rogalla from a French firm that had made the running in the development of aerated filters. Ironically a few years before the French designs came on to the market, Alan Wheatland at WPRL had demonstrated the feasibility of the process in a laboratory-scale column in which the filter medium Alan used was 6mm lengths of PVC tubing, 8mm in diameter, an account of this being published in our Annual Report for 1967 (i.e. in the middle of my period as Director). However at the time we discovered that a patent for the process was held though as far as I know never exploited by the firm of Albright & Wilson (Mfg) Ltd. Because of this and also because I thought that to produce a filter medium of the same style would be too expensive to use on full-scale, quite stupidly overlooking the now glaringly obvious possibility that a much cheaper granulated filter medium could be found, and that we could probably have made a 'deal' of some sort with Albright & Wilson, I failed to encourage Alan to press on with further research – yet another of my failings. Among other things I dimly recall was that we looked in preliminary fashion at the condition of the Chaopraha, the river flowing through the city which I had the pleasure of viewing from the steps out of the restaurant in one of the city's best hotels on the river bank.

Also although I cannot now precisely recall the context I remember on one day walking through the streets of the city with a dissolved-oxygen (DO) meter in my hand measuring the DO, of which there was precious little, in the very murky klongs (ditches for collecting drainage), bordering the riverside properties. This was an exercise in which one had to be nippy on one's feet to avoid being in collision with pedestrians, of whom there were many, or more seriously with vehicles in the dense traffic.

My final recollection is of being taken out to dinner at in my experience a unique restaurant in Bangkok, which I was told could accommodate up to 3000 diners. The floors were all boarded and meals and drinks were sometimes served by waiters moving (believe it or not) on roller-skates. There was also a splendid floorshow with lots of those captivating arm, hand and finger movements portrayed by the young ladies in the ensemble.

Sweden

The only visit I recall making to Sweden on behalf of the firm concerned a project David Cowie had initiated in Australia involving assessment of the potential of devices for dealing with domestic wastes other than by release to sewer. In this case I went to look at a Swedish unit that converted the waste from an individual house into a usable compost. Although this and other such devices undoubtedly worked and would be suitable for isolated rural dwellings they would not be economically viable for larger communities. One other albeit irrelevant recollection of either this trip or the previous one mentioned earlier is of forgetting that the time taken to get from the city centre in Stockholm to the airport is quite long and I was in any case already behind schedule when I reached the city terminal. I think the airline must have been alerted and possibly also because I was flying first class when I finally reached the airport I was whisked through all the formalities in no time and then directly on to the aircraft, which almost immediately took off. If only it were always so straightforward.

Japan

I have had only two visits to Japan and one was merely a one-night stopover in Tokyo. The other, accompanied by Kath, was to attend the 1992 IAWPR Conference in Kyoto. This afforded an opportunity to see something of the new sewage treatment plants in the area. These impressed me with the effectiveness of the measures taken to render the plants externally unobtrusive and largely free from odour. Kyoto itself and its Chion-in Temple, the Ichirike tea house and its geishas were fascinating and various other features such as the bullet-trains, the crowded streets in Tokyo and sushi and other food in the restaurants all made an impact.

On our return to the UK we had a stopover in Singapore and although I had been there on many business trips we managed to do one or two things that I had not done before. These included a round of golf on a 9-hole course near the hotel in which we stayed, a boat trip out of the harbour to one of the small islands not far away and getting a suit made, within 48 hours. In my opinion this suit was superior to any of the several suits I had had made to a similar timetable in Hong Kong and 12 years later it is still a favourite choice on the now relatively few occasions that I wear a suit.

Egypt

I first went to Egypt in the eighties to provide some input into the firm's initial efforts to compete for the design and supervision of construction for the proposed new wastewater treatment plant for Cairo. A little later I became Partner in Charge of our involvement in a joint project with other firms to evolve a Master Plan for the reconstruction of Port Said. In many ways our role in this interesting project was reasonably straightforward. My personal role was relatively minor, most of the leading effort being provided by David Kell, who later became a Partner and as it happens lives, not far away from our house, in Welwyn Garden City. Not unusually surviving memories relate not so much to the technical aspects as to largely irrelevant incidentals. One of these was being amazed that we did not suffer mishap when being taken back by car from Port Said to Cairo. This was because we were confronted on the journey by a seemingly endless stream of lorries and other traffic going in the opposite direction with blazing headlights forcing us on several occasions to take to the verges to avoid collision. Another irrelevancy was arriving in Cairo in the early hours of the morning in a flight from the Far East only to find that the Hilton Hotel where I had a booking had given my room to someone else. Fortunately as it happened David Kell had a flat in Cairo and was able to accommodate me.

After the Port Said project I provided a few other small inputs into the Cairo project, which was eventually awarded to a powerful combination of two UK firms, ours and John Taylor's, and two major US firms, Black & Veatch, and Camp Dresser and McKee. My abiding memory, again non-technical, is of attending the Son et Lumière presentation at the Pyramids, listening to the recorded commentary by Sir Laurence Olivier ('...I am Sphinx' etc) – and being badly bitten, as so often in similar circumstances, by mosquitoes. This was offset to some extent by an enjoyable meal at a hotel not far away and one I think is quite famous but whose name escapes me.

South Korea

Korea was yet another country where I spent only a short time. In conjunction with a Korean firm our UK firm was appointed by the Asian Development Bank to develop designs for upgrading water treatment plants in 21 towns to the south of Seoul. Because our water treatment (WT) department was in my domain I was designated Partner-in-Charge. The work was carried out locally by a team headed by one of the firm's Chief Engineers, the late David Ruxton, who had wide-ranging experience in various fields of water engineering, and staffed by members of the WT Department. Additional support was provided by engineers from the Korean firm. Initially matters appeared to be proceeding according to plan but after a while back in the UK I began to get signals from David indicating that we were in danger of going over budget and additional problems had arisen due to the Korean senior man sending staff originally allocated to the project to presumably more lucrative assignments in the Middle East. I went out to try to improve matters but got no further than arranging to meet with the ADB project manager and the Korean manager in London to try to resolve the difficulties. In the event this did not lead to anything of significant advantage to the firm and in the outcome we made a small, though to me none the less embarrassing, loss on the project.

Argentina

I went to Argentina on a 'prospecting mission' not long before the Falklands War. We had formed an association with a local firm, whose leader, Ricardo Bach, had arranged for me to give a series of lectures on wastewater treatment in Buenos Aires. These appeared to be reasonably well received but the Falklands War intervened before any hopes of obtaining significant work could be realized. Ricardo, with whom we maintained friendly relations throughout the war, was very hospitable, among other things taking me out to a club on the banks of a nearby river for an excellent lunch; and rather to my surprise to morning coffee at Harrods in Buenos Aires. Until that time I had no idea that there had been a connection with Harrods in the UK and I must say that the ambience in the Buenos Aires store was more than a touch reminiscent of that in the London store.

Taiwan

Taiwan was another country to which my only visit was in a job-prospecting capacity. In the early nineties I attended a meeting in

Taipei with one of the firm's senior staff, Richard Warren, in charge of prospecting in the region, plus representatives of a local firm with whom we had formed an alliance and senior officials involved in or connected with pollution control in Taiwan. Then subsequently I went on a tour of the main industrial areas in the country. We identified some possibilities for collaboration in pollution control projects but the circumstances seemed such that it would be some time before a specific opportunity developed to compete for one.

I enjoyed my short time in the country not least staying at the Sheraton hotel in Taipei. Richard got me enrolled as a member of the then Sheraton Club, which gave members staying in Sheraton hotels certain modest privileges. I took advantage of this soon after when I booked a golfing holiday with Kath at the Sheraton at Falesia in the Algarve, which as it happens has its own 9-hole course. We enjoyed ourselves so much that we have been there again every year since, usually either in the spring or late autumn. The Sheraton group merged with another US chain, Starwood, a few years ago but the membership privileges, as a now Starwood Preferred Guest, remain much the same and the excellent facilities at the hotel have continued to get even better.

Turkey

My first of only two visits to Turkey was to present two papers at a Conference on the 'Theory and Practice of Biological Wastewater Treatment' in 1976. This was organized by Professor Kriton Curi of Bogazici University and Wes Eckenfelder at a venue on the outskirts of Istanbul. The conference was sponsored by the NATO Advanced Study Institute. Unusually for me the two papers were largely 'ghost-written' by my colleague and co-author, David Kell, whom I mention elsewhere. By contrast not altogether unusual is the fact that I remember little of the conference itself, though I still have a volume of the Proceedings. Embarrassingly the two things I do remember were firstly being taken out to dinner at a restaurant where we were entertained at close quarters by voluptuous 'belly' dancers; and secondly, since the 'cold war' was on at the time, watching Russian naval vessels including an aircraft carrier moving through the Bosphorus in what seemed at the time somewhat menacing fashion.

A few years later the firm was appointed to design an outfall for effluent from a new pulp and paper mill located at Afyon about 400km south east of Istanbul. The effluent was to be well treated in a modern plant and discharged to a local lake. Our prime design objective was to avoid adverse impact on the waters of the lake. The lake was an isolated body of water bordered by only a few villages and in the local circumstances the design work was essentially that required for conveying the wastewater unobtrusively into the lake.

Again my memories are largely non-technical irrelevancies. One is of touring round the periphery of the lake and being very surprised to see adorning many of the quite primitive village properties a forest of television aerials. When I expressed my surprise I was told by the members of the Turkish team with whom we had formed an association for the project that it was the practice of many village men to go over to West Germany to work as casual labourers in order to earn enough to buy television sets. My other surprise was that Afyon was on the fringe of an opium poppy growing area and when walking from the paper mill to the lake, accompanied by a young engineer, he suddenly dashed into a field and returned with in his palm what looked to me just like Nescafé but was of course the contents of a crushed opium poppy. He then dipped a moistened finger into this and transferred it to his mouth. He invited me to do the same but I chickened out.

Philippines

In addition to the brief visit I made on the assessment of the needs for research into provision of water for small rural communities (mentioned earlier) I made several other visits to Manila in the Philippines in the late eighties and early nineties. On two early occasions I went or joined up with Tony Vail to meet with a local business lady with whom our Hong Kong firm had formed an association to foster that firm's job prospects in the country. In the course of these visits I gave three television interviews that she had kindly arranged. One of these presented me with some difficulty because I had arrived by one of the smaller jets (from, I think, Singapore), whose cabin pressure regulating system did not appear to be functioning perfectly; with the result that one ear had waxed up and I was partially deaf. Being interviewed on the box when in that condition is not to be recommended but I think that by keeping my 'good ear' pointed at the interviewer as best I could, I just about got away with it.

Though I had completely forgotten until my eye fell on a metal 'Plaque of Appreciation' hanging on the wall of my office I was the 'Resource Speaker' during a Seminar in 1984 organized by the Philippine Society of Sanitary Engineers Inc and held at the Asian Institute of Tourism, Quezon City.

In 1993 I joined a team from the firm under the general supervision of Richard Warren and led by Roger Brown, who contributed talks and papers to a Regional Consultation on Managing Water Resources to Meet Mega City Needs, organized by the Asian Development Bank in Manila. Case studies from eight developing mega cities (Bangkok, Beijing, Delhi, Dhaka, Jakarta, Karachi, Metro Manila and Seoul) were presented all of which were visited by Roger to provide preliminary guidance as to their contents. Over the years before the conference I had visited all of these cities bar Dhaka on other projects, so I knew something of the local problems. My role was simply to present a theme paper and take part in related discussions of this and other contributions. The paper was entitled 'Water, Pollution and Reuse'. The conference appeared to run smoothly and the proceedings were published in a well-presented volume of over 400 pages. However, to my mind the overriding problems in all the cities were not so much technical as shortage of finance.

My last visit to Manila was as a member of a team in another project obtained by Richard Warren. This was to advise staff of the Environmental Management board (of the Department of the Environment and Natural Resources) on water quality monitoring schemes and related topics. We stayed for most of the time at a quite new, well-appointed small hotel on the outskirts of Quezon City near the client's offices and laboratory, but owing to some over-booking Terry Heard (from the firm's water treatment department) and I had to spend some nights in a relatively primitive and cockroach-infested boarding house. Terry and I used to have a walk round the nearby urban area on most nights and then take dinner, which we invariably enjoyed, at local restaurants. On just one occasion I went up-market to one of the city's premier restaurants to have dinner with the HK firm's local liaison representative that I have mentioned earlier.

Kenya

Many of the flights to and from South Africa called en route into Nairobi, so I took the opportunity to investigate 'job prospects'. I managed to obtain only two quite small commissions. One was to provide some advice on effluent treatment to Kenya Canners, who had a large pineapple canning operation. The other was to offer similar advice to a fluoride mine, a short flight away from Nairobi. The fluoride mine was discharging wastewater into a river bordering the mine, causing local wags to allege that 'the crocodiles were afflicted with mottled teeth'. However neither of these initial contacts led to any significant projects.

When in Nairobi I stayed in the internationally well-known Norfolk Hotel, which a few years after my visits hit the headlines because a bomb was exploded on the premises, doing considerable damage. Regretfully I never got the chance to visit any of the main Safari areas, though I spent a pleasant half-day at a game park on the outskirts of Nairobi.

Switzerland

My visits to Switzerland were fairly few. One was to take part in a seminar and particularly to meet up with an old friend, regrettably now deceased, Dr Karl Wuhrmann, who had been conducting research in areas similar to those I was pursuing. I also went on at least two occasions (once with Kath) to the World Health Organization's (WHO's) HQ in Geneva to discuss activities of mutual interest (particularly in the early days) with Dr Pavanello, who organized the visit to India that I mention elsewhere.

When in Geneva I used to stay in a hotel opposite the end of Rue Mont Blanc, so-called I believe because on a clear day I was told you could just see the top of the mountain in the distance (though I never did). Among the strange things that seem to stick in my memory is going with Kath to a restaurant (I think on a bridge near one end of the Lake) and because Kath wanted the same thing ordering whatever it was 'pour deux'. Then of course I was mortified when the waiter brought one portion and two plates!

Although solely as the result of the 'French connection' let me just add, out of context, that this gaffe rivals two others that I made, one in Paris and one in Biarritz. In Paris ordering a meal in my schoolboy French by mistake I referred to Kath as *'mon mari'*. *'Oh non, Monsieur,'* said the waiter, *'Mon épousse'*, and then he added, *'Ou ma femme.'* In Biarritz I was contemplating ordering oysters and said to the waiter, 'Are they cooked?' 'Cooked', he said, 'Ugh, taste like chewing gum!'

Saudi-Arabia

Perhaps surprisingly I have never set foot in Saudi-Arabia despite having been Partner-in-charge of the design of lagoon systems for the treatment of the sewage for three holy cities including Mecca; and having a marginal supervisory responsibility for a project requiring assessment of the facilities likely to be necessary for treatment of wastewaters from oil refineries and petrochemical plants in a proposed new development in Jubail. In the case of the first project the fact is that I didn't have any notable expertise in the design of lagoons and the staff we had on-site were perfectly capable of completing the work satisfactorily without any input from me.

The second project was slightly bizarre in that it required essentially hypothetical forecasts of requirements for wastewaters that at that time didn't exist. For this reason the work was mainly done in the UK and because of his relevant expertise was largely organized and conducted by Colin Appleyard.

Chile

I went to Chile on only one occasion this being in the early 1980s. My role was to advise scientific personnel, appointed by the local firm with whom we had formed an association, on water quality aspects of a World Bank project to examine the scope for introducing a dam into the River Aconcagua, which flows through Santiago, to enable impounded water to be conveyed to two rivers further north. These rivers, which were drawn on to irrigate the fruit and vegetable growing areas through which they flowed, often dried up during the hotter times of the year.

My flight into Santiago from some other overseas project was considerably delayed and I think it was around midnight when we landed. I waited in the arrivals area expecting to be met by the firm's project engineer in local charge, Brian Cox, or one of his staff, but gradually all the other passengers drifted away and I was left on my own until a member of the airport personnel came up and said, 'Is your name Downing?' When I said that it was he then said that, 'I have to tell you that because of a midnight curfew Mr Cox cannot come to collect you.' However, he said, 'We do have specially licensed taxis one of which will take you to your destination.' I duly got in the cab but was slightly alarmed when as we reached the outskirts of the city we were stopped by an armed military guard unit. However the driver produced a pass and I waved my British passport and we were allowed on our way. When we reached the house that Brian Cox and his wife Doris were occupying I found that Doris was suffering quite badly from 'flu. However they still contrived to ensure that this didn't affect the programme they had mapped out for me and after a day or two of technical discussions I went off on a tour of the river systems with a local scientist involved in the project. This wasn't quite as straightforward as I might have expected as there had been quite extensive local flooding and some of the roads we had intended to take were flooded. However we went alongside the Aconcagua towards the coast past the industrial city of Valparaiso, and then into the attractive resort of Vina del Mar, which among other things had some Las Vegas style casinos. The following day we toured the river valleys further north seeing, in passing, many vineyards which I imagine were the source of the many excellent Chilean wines that are nowadays on the UK market.

On returning to Santiago I met up with one of the Partners of the local firm whose name to my embarrassment I cannot remember. He was a very interesting man who according to local informants had allegedly 'broken every bone in his body', mostly playing polo. I believe his skill at that sport was considerable and he had brought teams over to the UK to play against home teams, including members of the Royal Family. He was also a useful golfer and he kindly took Brian Cox and me for a round that we much enjoyed at the Santiago Country Club.

I cannot now recall what the water quality issues that I commented on were but in a sense this was ultimately irrelevant because the conclusions of the study were that increased revenue from improved irrigation of crops would be insufficient to outweigh the cost of the dam.

By the time I came to take my return flight I had been abroad quite some time and was keen to return to the UK as swiftly as possible. At this point I conceived the reprehensible idea of taking a flight to Miami (by Aeroperu or Lanchile, I forget which) and then picking up Concorde for the last lap to the UK. I thought that if my Partners objected, as they probably would have, I could pay the additional costs above the first class fare myself. However I was saved from this abject indiscretion though not in a manner that I would have wished. What happened was that less than about an hour after taking-off from Santiago the pilot came through on the intercom to tell us that he'd been informed that there was a bomb on board! He therefore turned round and headed back to Santiago as quickly as possible. When we arrived there, fortunately safe and sound, all the luggage was taken out and spread across the tarmac so that a rigorous search could be conducted. In the event nothing was found and after two or three hours we were on our way again. By the time we arrived in the States Concorde had long gone and I think I arrived home about a day later than had been my original intention.

However, quite a few years later, Kath and I did manage on one of her birthdays to take a short Concorde flight from Heathrow over the Bay of Biscay. I recall that we had lunch in two parts, the first course on the ground and the rest in the air. The plane did go supersonic for a short period and I'm glad we had the experience, particularly as the aircraft is now 'no more'.

Other Countries

Other countries that I visited for very brief periods were Zimbabwe, Greece, Jordan and Canada. I went to Salisbury (now Harare) in Zimbabwe when it was still Rhodesia just before 'decolonization' to assess the status of the pollution control technology in the country and related work prospects. My chief memory is of visiting a sewage treatment plant, I hope for the one and only time with an armed escort, and being told en route that in the then current state of unrest there had been incidents of roads being mined. Fortunately my trip passed without incident.

Breaking a journey to or from much farther afield I called in at Athens to meet with a representative of a local firm, again to assess prospects for collaboration. Sadly nothing came of this but I suppose as a kind of compensation I was taken on a quick trip to view the Acropolis and the Parthenon.

I went to Amman in Jordan, again in course of a visit elsewhere, simply to provide a small snippet of advice on a pollution control project in which the firm was engaged there.

My visit to Canada, where I went with Kath, was primarily to take a holiday. However there was a business element in that I arranged the trip to coincide with the IAWPRC's biennial International Conference that was taking place in Vancouver. I did so because I wanted to meet up again with Wes Eckenfelder to explain more fully the reasons that I had felt unable to take up his kind invitation to lecture once more in the courses that he had arranged for the Conference. Our trip began in Vancouver about a week before the start of the Conference and progressed on through Vancouver Island, then by boat up to I think Prince Rupert (and including a whale watching excursion) and then by train (initially the Rocky Mountaineer) round to Lake Louise and Banff, and then back via Kamloops to Vancouver. This was an altogether splendid trip through fabulous scenery and many interesting sites, much enhanced by the local knowledge of our excellent lady guide 'Happy Feather', who as her name implies had Inuit forebears. When we got back to Vancouver I went to the Conference Centre, only to find that Wes had not been well and had been unable to come. I hope to catch up with him again before too long.

CHAPTER 9

1996 – The Present

AFTER RETIREMENT, apart from this present exercise, I had only one further engagement that required drawing on my professional experiences. This involved giving a somewhat jocular talk at a meeting of the 5Ss at the Coleshill Treatment Plant, near Birmingham, on the evolution of sewage treatment processes over the period from 1913 to 1996. It was a jolly occasion, bringing me into contact with many old friends, especially including Frank Sanderson, originally a Director of one of the leading wastewater treatment equipment manufacturers, Ames Crosta Mills Ltd, whom I had not seen for several years.

However this was just a brief foray into the past. Apart from playing more golf and taking many more holidays and short breaks retirement has enabled Kath and me to get together a little more frequently with most of the surviving members of the family, my (half) sister Margaret and her son John (Dr John Akeroyd), and other (half) nephews and nieces Patty and Henry Jelley and Richard and Zazie Carruthers. John Akeroyd is a notable botanist, the author of several books, and as I learned very recently has just returned from a visit to Romania where he has been assisting Prince Charles with a horticulture project. Richard and Zazie share our enthusiasm for golf and we have had some good games together both on their course at North Stoke, near Wallingford, and at ours at Knebworth.

As usual, early in this phase I made another of my blunders. This time I allowed myself to be 'seduced' by a firm that claimed that notable investment advisers, such as Morgan Stanley, had reported that an investment in Scotch whisky might well appreciate in value by around 18 percent per annum. Foolishly instead of asking for more details I went ahead and bought two Hogsheads of a single malt, Tomatin, said to be favoured by the Japanese. It soon transpired that among many others I had been conned, the market value of the Scotch being a good deal less than I had paid, and selling it in relatively small quantities being quite difficult. Several of my leg-pulling friends said recently that I might get a reasonable-sized readership for these Memoirs if I gave away a bottle of Tomatin with each copy. However as any readers who have bought a copy will now be perhaps ruefully aware, I have so far resisted that 'advice'.

Following this incident my most dominant activity has been my involvement in Stevenage PROBUS Club. As the acronym implies PROBUS is a club for Professional and Business persons (though wags would have it that the members are 'Poor Retired Old Buggers Useless Sexually').

I believe from talking with members of other PROBUS clubs that ours in Stevenage has one of the most, if not the most, diverse and intensive annual programme of any in the country. Briefly we have two lunches every month, in most months a walk usually of about 5 miles in the country, though occasionally over shorter distance in London or Hertfordshire towns, and again in most months a day excursion to a site with interesting features. Additionally we have a walking holiday of 3-4 days, a spring holiday of similar duration, a main autumn holiday of 7-8 days, two golf matches and a bowls match, plus visits to the horse races at Towcester and the dogs at Walthamstow, and usually before Christmas to the Thursford Spectacular or the Albert Hall or the Barbican.

Mentioning Walthamstow reminds me that our annual visit affords me the opportunity to meet again with two splendid friends who come as guests, Brian and Sheila Richardson. Brian and I used to play golf together quite frequently in the early nineties but he subsequently gave up the game in favour of other pursuits especially those involving their beloved pointer dogs (of which they have four). Brian did me one of the best favours I have ever had. As MD of a major mutual insurance company he used to change his company car at intervals of roughly three years. As it happened on one of these occasions, I was thinking of changing my vehicle (a BMW) which was eight years old and had been 'written off' by our firm (B & P). Brian said that his firm usually settled for Glass's trade-in price and if I cared to pay that I could have it. The car was, and indeed still is, a splendid 4.2 Jaguar Sovereign, which had then done only about 30,000 miles. I said yes right away and have been delighted with my purchase ever since. It is now eighteen years old but has done only just over 90,000 miles and still looks very respectable (but, I hasten to add, is not up for sale).

A year or two after joining I was inveigled into taking office on the Committee as Assistant Entertainments Officer and in the following year Entertainments Officer. I then went on to be Vice-Chairman and ultimately Chairman in 2001-2. I reckon that in my Chairman's year I spent about 80 days on PROBUS activities. I enjoyed every, well nearly every, minute of it and I look forward to continuing in the Club for at least a few more years. One thing that greatly pleased me was that during my term on the Committee my three friends and former colleagues, George Eden, Arthur Boon and Alan Bruce, all joined the Club. Furthermore Arthur and Alan are now both very active members of the Committee.

As usual I perpetrated a mishap of a sort. This occurred in 1999, my first year as Entertainments Officer when I had arranged for the first time in the Club an overseas holiday travelling by air, in this case to Dublin and other delightful venues in and around Cork, Waterford and Killarney. Unfortunately I had developed angina and arrangements were made for me to have a triple heart by-pass at Harefield Hospital. However by ill luck this took place shortly before the trip to Ireland and I could not go. The good side to this event was that no trauma was involved. I was taken to an anteroom next to the operating theatre on a Monday evening and was told to take two white pills which would make me feel drowsy. After taking them I don't remember a thing until wakening at about 6 a.m. the following morning feeling quite relaxed and without pain. Things progressed so well that I was home by midday the following Friday and except for two short bouts of fibrillation I have had no adverse after effects.

The second of these fibrillations occurred about three years ago on a Friday after two or three hours of probably over-vigorous leaf sweeping. By the following day my heartbeat was still rather irregular and because Kath and I were booked to go on a golfing holiday to our favourite hotel in the Algarve on the Monday I rang my GP. As it was the weekend my call was switched to a stand-by emergency unit in Luton. I was put on to a Dr Ganguly who turned out to be the uncle of the Indian Test batsman. In response to my query he said, 'Oh no I shouldn't go if I were you.' Regrettably we cancelled the holiday and my insurance claim was turned down because when renewing the policy earlier in the year I failed to remember that I should have notified the Company that I had had the by-pass. Aside from this I could not help but reflect that if the technology and skill made available to me had been available in my father's day he might have lived a good deal longer.

Another enjoyable facet of this last period has been taking a short golfing holiday with two close friends, from Knebworth G C and PROBUS, Roy and Mavis Porritt, at Des Ormes, near Dol de Bretagne in Brittany. So far we have done the trip, usually in June, by road, taking the cars across on Brittany Ferries (two cars being necessary because of the amount of golfing clobber that we need). There are many other good courses within easy road-driving distance of Des Ormes and we have played a good many of them. We have also sampled with satisfaction the fare at several restaurants and crêperies in the area. We also have frequent get-togethers with other regular golfing partners and their wives, especially Harry and Jo Shields and Vic and Lina Smith. Additionally we meet regularly with Audrey Woodhead, whose late husband Geoffrey (a senior BP man in his working days) was another of my golfing friends.

Mentioning PROBUS yet again reminds me that on our Christmas outing last year to the Thursford Spectacular we went into the bar at the interval and who should be standing there, complete with cloth cap, but Fred Dibnah. I said, 'I thought I recognized you,' to which he replied, 'Aye, once seen, never forgotten.' Being as it were fellow northerners we had a couple of minutes of pleasant chat with him. We were thus very pleased to learn shortly afterwards that in the New Year's Honours he had been awarded an OBE.

This triggers another recollection in somewhat similar mode. This concerns the fact that in 2002 Kath and I were delighted to get an invitation from the Master of Sidney Sussex College, Professor Sandra Dawson, to dine with her in Hall and stay overnight in the Master's Lodge (she had kindly been made aware of my existence by Gwilym Roberts). This was a thoroughly enjoyable and for me quite nostalgic event. It was a kind of fitting prelude to the great pleasure we had when learning that in the New Year's Honours Sandra Dawson had become Dame Sandra.

Well, I hope to get a few more pleasant experiences before I depart the scene – but sufficient unto the day.

Index of People

Fernie, Geoff 126
Fish, Sir Hugh 135
Flaxman, E W (Ted) 68, 94, 106, 111, 128
Ford, S H (Stanley) 98, 147
Frost, Edward 18
Frost, George 18

Gale, Dr R S (Bob) 48
Game, Ralph 28
Gameson, A L H (Hugh) 106
Ganguly, Dr 187
Gardiner, Jack 147
George, Alan 136
Gerrard, R T (Ronald) 118
Goad, J E J (Jeremy) 170
Goodman, Albert 116
Goronzy, Merv 151
Graveney, Tom 4
Gray, Sally 8
Griffiths, Sir Eldon 62, 97, 101, 117
Groves, Dr Ray 112, 113

Hagger, Mike 141
Hailsham, Lord 63-4
Hamlin, Professor M J 118-19
Hancock, Sheila 127
Harremoës, Professor Poul 118
Hart, Ian 22
Hawksworth, Fred 8
Hay, Alex 8
Healey, D A (Dave) 101
Heard, Terry 178
Herber, Keith 75
Hetherington, J S (James) 121
Hewson, John 52
Hicks, Ron 161
Holdgate, Sir Martin 5, 110, 169
Holmes, Paul 149
Hopwood, Adrian 35
Hooi, Kah Hung 154
Howarth, Bill 5
Hoyle, B G (Brian) 75
H R H The Princess Anne 112
Hutton, Len 10

Imhoff, Karl 118

Jacklin, Tony 67
Jackson, Chris 52
Jackson, Claire 75, 114
Jackson, Peter 7
James, Dr A N (Tony) 105, 108, 152, 153
Jeger, Mrs Lena 62, 63, 64
Jelley, Henry and Patty 184
Jenkins, Dr S H (Sam) 57
Johnson, Nora 53
Jones, Dr Gordon 45, 46

Kanwisher, John 30
Kaye, Danny 146
Kell, A D K (David) 143, 173, 175
Key, Dr Arthur 58
Kickuth, Professor 113
Kinmount, Alex 141
Kirby, T K M (Mick) 5
Knowles, George 35, 44
Koch, Pierre 118
Kountz, Professor Rupert 30
Kubo, Dr Takeshi 150
Kullenberg, Professor G 169

Laing 40
Lang, Marty and Bertha 102
Laver, Rod 17
Leclerc, Professor Edmond 26
Leighton, Lord 1
Lester, Fred 93, 98
Lillee, Dennis 126
Lines, Gordon 52
Lister, A R 56
Longwell, Dr J 15
Lowden, George 14, 22
Lowry, Lady (Barbara) 104
Lui, Mr 117
Lund, Dr John 123
Lupton, A R (Arthur) 149
Lyons, Joe 70, 71

Macdonald, David 135
Marais, Professor G V R 144

Vail, Tony 146, 149, 177
Van der Post, John 114

Wall, Max 8
Wallingford, F E (Frank) 75
Warren, Richard 104, 175, 177, 178
Welch, Denis and Barbara 26
Wheatland, A B (Alan) 170
Will, Peter 4
Williams, Shirley (later Baroness) 64
Wilson, Harold 64

Wolf, Professor Peter 119
Wood, Dr Frank 147
Woodhead, Geoffrey and Audrey 187
Wran, Neville 124
Wuhrmann, Karl 179

Yang, Daniel 134, 135

Zhang, Min 139
Zuckermann, Sir Solly (later Lord) 59,
   64

Index of Places, Projects
and Organizations

Lahore 166
Lake Burrinjuck, Australia 123
Lake Tahoe, California 66
Lake Taupo, New Zealand 160
Lake Trawsfynydd, Wales 14, 116
Lavernock Point, Wales 99
Liège 26
Lima 120, 122
Lisbon 41
Local Government Operational
    Research Unit 63
Lok on Pai, Hong Kong 80, 101, 147
Long Term Water Research
    Requirements Committee 110
Longton, Staffordshire 1
Lough Neagh 109, 129
Lower Molonglo (Water Treatment
    Plant) 102
Lucky Mac Mine, Utah 125
Lyallpur, Pakistan 166
Lytton Arms, Old Knebworth 25

Malaysia 134, 154-7
Manhattan College, New York 29
Manila 76, 176-8
Mars Ltd 13
Massachusetts Institute of Technolgy
    (MIT), Boston 9, 29
Maunsell & Partners 126, 128
Mauritius 167-8
Mautai 139
Mecca 179
Melbourne 67, 122, 124, 125, 127
Mi Yun Reservoir 135-6
Michaelis constant 35
Milan 60
Ming Tombs 140
Ministry of Agriculture fisheries and
    Food (MAFF) 15, 17, 25
Ministry of Housing and Local
    Government 49, 62, 66
Ministry of Technology 68
Moelenstraat, The Hague 43
Monterey 153
Montreal 76
Muar Basin, Malaysia 155

Munich, IAWPR Conference 45

Nagpur, India 76
Nairobi 178
Napier-Hastings, New Zealand 159
Nashville, Tennessee 117
National Aeronautics and Space
    Administration (NASA) 150
Nature 22
New Civil Engineer 53, 105
New Orleans 150
New South Wales State Pollution
    Control Commission 122
New York 28, 150-1
New Zealand 159-61
Newton's Law of Cooling 25
Ninham Shand & Partners 140
Nitrification and nitrifying bacteria 119,
    149
Node, Codicote 40
North Atlantic Treaty Organization
    (NATO) 48, 169

Organization for European
    Cooperation and Development
    (OECD) 48, 58, 126
Ottawa 76
Overseas Development Administration
    (ODA) 133, 134, 135

Pakistan 75-6, 166-7
Palmerston North, NZ 128, 161
Park Hotel De Zalm, The Hague 43
Pearl River Estuary 139
Pebble Beach, California 153
Peninsula Hotel, Hong Kong 146
Penrhyndeudraeth 14
Pergamon Press 110
Permutit Co Ltd 9
Perth, Australia 109, 112, 125, 128-9, 169
Peru 120-2
Philippine Society of Sanitary
    Engineers Symposium 1984 177
Philippines 76, 176-8
POLMET '85 Conference in Hong
    Kong 149